DISPATCHES FROM UKRAINE
TACTICAL MEDIA REFLECTIONS AND RESPONSES
EDITED BY
MARIA VAN DER TOGT
AND 11111 &23%#719

Theory on Demand #44
Dispatches from Ukraine—Tactical Media Reflections and Responses

Edited by Maria van der Togt and 11111 &23%#719.

Copy edited by Chloë Arkenbout, proofread by Laurence Scherz

Authors: Elmaz Asan, Franco 'Bifo' Berardi, Andrii Dostliev, Lia Dostlieva, Olexii Kuchanskyi, Karyna Lazaruk, Geert Lovink, Lera Malchenko, Svitlana Matviyenko, Maria Plichta, Ellen Rutten, Maria van der Togt, Marc Tuters, Michał 'rysiek' Woźniak

Cover design: Katja van Stiphout
Design and production: Maria van der Togt and 11111 &23%#719

Publisher: Institute of Network Cultures, Amsterdam, 2022

ISBN print-on-demand: 9789492302861
ISBN EPUB: 9789492302878

Contact
Institute of Network Cultures
Email: info@networkcultures.org
Web: http://www.networkcultures.org

Download this publication free of charge or order a copy at http://networkcultures.org/publications.

institute of
network cultures

waag🅜futurelab

Dedicated to all those who have been affected by war

CONTENTS

Tactical Media Room

Informational Export

INTRODUCTION

MARIA VAN DER TOGT, GEERT LOVINK AND 11111 &23%#719

Welcome to Tactical Media Room Ukraine

Tactical Media Room (TMR) is an initiative of Waag Futurelab and the Institute of Network Cultures (Amsterdam University of Applied Sciences) in Amsterdam. The project was founded late February 2022, right after the Russian invasion of Ukraine, and facilitates weekly (hybrid) meetings. The platform consists of hackers, artists, journalists, activists, designers and researchers, both known and anonymous, in the Netherlands and elsewhere. A Signal group of currently forty members addresses topics and activities that vary from disinformation, censorship and propaganda research to mapping platform geopolitics, support regarding hardware and online services by ISPs and hosting providers, tech knowledge exchanges (from satellite phones to cybersecurity) and practical aid support. Its concrete aim is to coordinate and support independent tactical media, journalists, newsrooms and civic initiatives in and from Ukraine, as well as to analyze the media stances upon which current Russian and Belarusian propaganda is built. These activities and discussions are made public through a monthly public program, lectures, and exhibitions, a blog and a weekly newsletter. This Theory on Demand is an overview of the most important outcomes from the period between March-July 2022.

Tactical Media Room unites critical thinkers and cultural workers across Europe. The driving force behind TMR is first and foremost to support tactical media, and not exclusively, to Ukrainian people at risk. We do so in the awareness that the war is, placing vast amounts of Ukrainian journalists, media activists, artists, and scholars at acute risk in one way or another. Belarusian and Russian critical thinkers, however, are also at risk and in need of support. Ukrainian people who face or flee the war deal with different problems and needs than Belarusian and Russian critical thinkers who deal with political persecution because they express dissent against authorities. TMR aims to support both of these groups.

The start of TMR goes back to an informal meeting late February, where members of Waag and the Institute of Network Cultures gathered at Waag in Amsterdam. Free Russia and the ISP Freedom Internet started to discuss the media/digital aspect of the war and how activists could respond. In part this was done by the same people that founded Press Now back in 1992, the Dutch support campaign for independent media in former Yugoslavia. Press Now operated from an upstairs room at Amsterdam cultural centre De Balie, next to the room where the non-profit internet community provider De Digitale Stad launched in January 1994. A place where later that same year The Waag Society for Old and New Media was also born, before it moved to its historical building, right in the centre of Amsterdam. And, last but not least, the place where the tactical media festival *The Next Five Minutes* had its offices, an event series kicked off in January 1993 in the neighboring cultural venue Paradiso that initially used the phrase 'tactical television'. Thirty years later Amsterdam looks radically different: gentrified, expensive, a tech hub for companies like Adyen, Booking and WeTransfer. Yet, the necessity to respond to what is happening in Ukraine is in the same spirit as these pioneers and was immediately felt, across generations and communities.

What's at stake here? What do we discuss? Unlike tactical media in the 1990s this is not about free radio, video distribution, independendant magazines, and bulletin board systems. In 2022 media solidarity organizes itself via Telegram groups, Twitter accounts, and yes, still email, in a desperate attempt to catch up with news of the shellings and movements of friends and other refugees. As Olexii Kuchansky describes in his contribution, there was a widely experienced feeling of a body, not as an individual human organism, but rather as a network of individual relationships and interactions, as a tension between the individual and its environment. "In this sense, a conglomeration of selves united by a common territory form a multiple body—a shared membrane where fear, pain, and hope spread from Mariupol, Kharkiv, and Kherson to Lviv and Uzhhorod, and now also to Warsaw, Krakow, Berlin, and Bucharest, and back." This correlation is at the same time deeply timeless, yet current and related to high-tech, geo-politics, drones, and live broadcasting via smartphones. Consequently, this provokes an instant need to question the barrage of images: is it fake news or not? We have to believe our eyes, yet the sheer spectacle of destruction also induces numbness.

About this publication

With this collection we aim to gather various expertise around tactical media that exists within our network. Let this Theory on Demand be a repository for knowledge around tactical media—an introduction, and an invitation for anyone who is interested in the topic. The purpose of this collection is to develop an active resource that can be utilized to connect current practices in tactical media, while maintaining a living archive of past practices. We hope this publication can be the start of an ever-growing exchange of knowledge and we kindly invite all those with an interest in the topic to reach out.

All the featured authors track the effects of a warfront intertwined with the digital realm. Networks are never merely tools. These hyper-sensitive environments are subjected to constant mutation; formed by the negotiations of people(s) and institutions. Questioned, destroyed, argued, and sublimated through an ever-growing information stream.

The publication starts with insights into the public programs organized by TMR in the past months and introduces some of the initiatives of its members. The series of meetups opened with a public discussion in the Makers Guild at Waag Society between Belarusian activist from the Belarusian opposition movement in the Netherlands Ilya Shcharbitski, an analyst in the Ukrainian office of Argus Media Victoria Dovgal, and the publisher of The *Moscow Times* Alexander Gubsky. Together, they exchanged their experiences with dis- and misinformation produced by Russian propagandist media before and during the 2022 war. According to Dovgal, the most powerful tool to fight propaganda and disinformation is education, which is an especially urgent issue due to an insurmountable number of educational institutions that have been bombed in Ukraine since February. To support the point about the importance of education, Ellen Rutten, whose essay is also included here, presented the initiative—the University of New Europe—that aims at helping scholars at risk from the region.

The second meetup was a special solidarity screening conducted with the Emergency Support Initiative of Kyiv Biennial and HomeCinema. The screening featured a series of works filmed by moving image artists based in Ukraine. All of the works were created in February and spring 2022, giving a raw and immediate insight into the filmmakers' current practices. The films blatantly remind us of the importance of filmmaking in times of crisis and the necessity to make visible and keep traces as acts of resistance. The list of the featured artists is published in this Theory on Demand.

The third meetup organized by TMR extended initial debates between between two camps—the Internet Freedom supporters, who stand for freedom of expression, and the Freedom of Press followers, who insist on propaganda censorship. For this publication, Maria Plichta wrote a report on the debate that happened in the Amsterdam academic debating centre Spui25 on June 30, 2022, highlighting the most prominent points and arguments. All together, the descriptions and reflections on the TMR meetings make up part one of this publication.

The name of the second part, Informational Export, stems from Sophia Kornienko's analysis of the stances upon which propaganda is built. In her essay, Sophia states that the main source of Russian export is 'the idea that there is no truth.' The articles that follow denounce, in one way or another, the way information circulates in the digital age embraced by war. Italian theorist Franco 'Bifo' Berardi discusses how the ongoing war that Russia initiated in Ukraine is different than other wars and what role fake news and politically charged information play in it. This essay is followed by the text of TMR members Karyna Lazaruk and Marc Tuters who elaborate on fake news and so-called 'open source intelligence' OSINT-technologies and the way in which they are appropriated by propagandist media. Michał 'rysiek' Woźniak explains why the analysis of fake news should not be limited to focusing on legislation only. 'We should instead be looking closely at how it is possible that it spreads so fast (and who benefits from this),' he says. 'We should be finding ways to fix the media funding crisis; and we should be making sure that future generations receive the mental tools that would allow them to cut through biases, hoaxes, rhetorical tricks, and logical fallacies weaponized to wage information wars.' Lia Dostlieva and Andrii Dostliev address the ways in which culture is being utilized as a powerfull tool of state propaganda in 'Not All Criticism is Russophobic: on Decolonial Approach to Russian Culture.' The article questions what Russian voices can bring into public discussions and offers guides for a non-imperialistic way of thinking and acting. Part two ends with the speech by Elmaz Asan, a Ukrainian jounalist and a representative of the indigenous Crimean Tatar people, delivered at 'The European Internet Blockade of Russian Propagandist Media' event at Spui25 in which she touches upon the colonial nature of Russian journalism and propaganda.

Part three consists of essays united under the title 'War Mentality/Digitality', which provides a personal account of the war and its seepage into the digital—zooming in on digital war tactics, but also on the experience of a war largely observed and mediated through the online. Svitlana Matviyenko and Geert Lovink reflect on the origin and wider context of the diary Svitlana has been publishing since late February 2022 on the Institute of Network Cultures website. Before the Russian invasion started, Geert contacted Svitlana to ask her how she was estimating the large scale Russian exercises and build-up at the border. On February 21 she responded: 'I have been writing a diary since early January. I call it *Dispatches from the Place of Imminence*, in which I am trying to reflect on the situation, and particularly, the cyber warfare side of it.' In the text 'Digital Leviathan and His Nuclear Tail: Notes on Body and The Earth in The State of War,' Olexii Kuchanskyi describes a corporeal experience of war through a united and multiple body, where the body functions as 'a network of relationships and interactions', and as 'a tension between the individual and its environment.' Lera Malchenko text, "I Notice the Extension", is a nod to Marshall McLuhan's *Understanding Media: The Extensions of Man.* She dissects the boundaries of a body as it gets increasingly intermixed in a complex heterogeneous system as a result of war. The section ends with one of Svitlana Matviyenko's *Dispatches From the Place of Imminence.* In this particular entry from the diary series (part 10 from May 31, 2022) she unpacks imperialist epistemology through media theory and political analysis, carefully interlacing the subject with personal accounts of the absurd and the banal.

The publication rounds up with a list of sources and Initiatives to Support Ukraine, Ukrainian Refugees, and People at Risk.

TACTICAL MEDIA ROOM

TACTICAL MEDIA MEETUP #1: HOW TO NAVIGATE THE (DIS)INFORMATION LANDSCAPE

Reflexions on Navigating (Dis)information

MARIA VAN DER TOGT

We met around eight, on a Thursday evening.[1] Welcomed by the smell of homemade soup. Courtesy of Mirror Soup Kitchen Lviv. Hackers, artists, researchers, journalists, and passerby's filled their bellies with the very same soup that's providing essential sustenance a mere 1,362 km away. The very same recipe, cooked on the very same day. It tasted delicious, though a little sad, and warm in many ways.[2]

Marleen Stikker moved towards the front of the crowd. Her words made public what had long been in the making. In late February 2022, a group of like-minded Netherlands-based media specialists came together to support independent tactical media, journalists, newsrooms, and civic initiatives in Ukraine, Belorussia, and Russia. Together they formed the Tactical Media Room.

The word 'tactic' finds its origin in the modern Latin *tactica* (17c.) and from the Greek *taktike techne,* meaning 'the art of arrangement'. Specifically pertaining to tactics in war— the order or disposition of an army. The root of the word comes from 'to touch, or to handle'.

I'm reminded of Putin's fatty fingers softly tapping on his desk
So easy to despise[3]

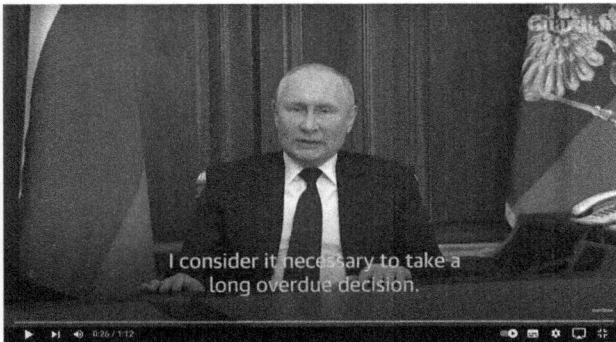

I consider it necessary to take a
long overdue decision.

---

1   Waag | Tactical Media Meetup #1: How to navigate the (dis)information landscape. (2022, April). Waag. https://waag.org/en/event/tactical-media-meetup-1-how-navigate-disinformation-landscape/.
2   Mirror Soup Kitchen. (2022). [Instagram Profile]. Instagram. https://www.instagram.com/mirrorsoupkitchen/.
3   Putin signs decree recognising Ukraine's two breakaway regions. (2022, February 21). [Video]. YouTube. https://www.youtube.com/watch?v=jUkrigz3L0Q&t=27s.

But it is more than the mere weaponization of the media.
There is an inherent shift—relations change in reverberation.
A move from being subjected to media to becoming its very object.

One of the things Marleen says stays with me particularly. "TMR is not a collective of organizations. It's a coming together of individuals that bring a network."
A web of nodes with a collective urgent agency.[4]

Kristina Petrasova welcomes Alexander Gubsky and Ilya Shcharbitski to the stage. Respectively the publisher of *The Moscow Times*, and a civil activist and spokesperson of the Belarusian opposition movement in the Netherlands.

We talk about changing perceptions, in Ukraine, but also in Belarus and Russia. We discept some of the strategies of Putin's dictatorship and chokehold on information.
We discuss the many lives subjected to the echo of words and formulas dictated by the Russian state.
And how somehow   Lie + lie + lie + lie + lie   equals a thick vacuum
Of rigidly controlled public space

Our brief guide through the disturbing (dis)information landscape is followed by a positive forward-looking announcement: Ellen Rutten presents the University of New Europe. She, and many colleagues with her, recognize a lack of equality and educational standards in Europe for its citizens and refugees, and want to raise funds to be able to train disadvantaged students, with a special focus on those parts of Europe where intellectual freedom is at risk. They aim to fill the gap created by political repression against the leading East-European institutions of higher learning. Find out more about the initiative here; https://neweurope.university[5].

We settle deeper into our subject.

В озере лжи много мертвой рыбы
In the lake of lies, there are many dead fish[6]

Boris Noordenbos takes to the stage. He spearheads a discussion on the role of historical narratives and conspiracies in Russian Propaganda.

We look at a series of misplaced images
Sustaining the most mythologized of narratives[7]

4   Referencing Karen Barad's Agential Agency.
5   *neweurope – mission statement*. (2022). UNE. https://neweurope.university
6   Russian proverb
7   Propaganda war image. (2022, May 4). [Video]. Vimeo. https://vimeo.com/706034606.

Video still, propagada video's, Vimeo

*THESE WAR GLORIFYING IMAGES ARE STAGED, can't believe that requires clarification

I think along with Sylvia Wynter,
Who once so eloquently explained the power of narration,[8]
We humans are a unique alchemical storytelling species: the stories we tell literally
transform us both physically, genetically, and socially.

It's funny, Haraway taught me to love SF[9]
But they completely destroy it.

I'm reminded of an article by Elvia Wilk in Artforum on Ecosystemic Fiction.[10]
'Fake news creates real news'. Alluding to the power of fiction to intervene in reality. In the
current political climate, there is barely a needle-pin gap between conspiracy theory and
state policy.

We're stuck in a downward spiral of self-fulfilling prophecies from hell.
A fictional turned non-fictional land where the global LGBTQ+ movement is a plot against
Russia, Ukraine is preparing bio weapons and the West is eagerly scheming to carve up
Russia's territory. All the while Hollywood is working hard to produce the scenes used to
discredit Russia.[11]

These battles of words are shedding real blood.

---

8   Mckittrick, K. (2015). Sylvia Wynter (1ste editie). Amsterdam University Press.
9   Haraway, D. J. (2016). Staying with the Trouble. Amsterdam University Press.
10   Wilk, E. (2021, January 7). Elvia Wilk on ecosystemic fiction. Artforum International. https://www.
     artforum.com/books/elvia-wilk-on-ecosystemic-fiction-84860#:%5C%7E:text=In%20response%20
     to%20ecosystemic%20upheaval,flips%20the%20roles%20of%20actor.
11   Yablokov, I. (2022, 25 april). Opinion | Russia's Putin Now Seems to Believe Conspiracy Theories. The
     New York Times. https://www.nytimes.com/2022/04/25/opinion/putin-russia-conspiracy-theories.html

We live in a conspiratorial reality where fiction is being utilized as an ideological vessel.[12]
Always a generation behind reality.

We must reconnect what words have separated.

I just don't know how
Instead, I offer a quote from Etel Adnan:

Writing that requiem I had to hear the representative of those humans who claim that they
are tired of the world's situation and that they will be looking for a new Revelation. But the
choir kept telling them that Revelation is indivisible. It's one. It's very likely what was meant
by Nietzsche when he mentioned the eternal return of the same.

Night functions like the snow. Erases the landscape.[13]

12   Copley, C. (z.d.). Conspiratorial Reality and Ecosystemic Fiction, an interview with Elvia Wilk. Schemas
     of Uncertainty. http://schemasofuncertainty.com/conspiratorial-reality-and-ecosystemic-fiction-an-
     interview-with-elvia-wilk.
13   Adnan, E. (2020). Shifting the Silence. Adfo Books.https://vimeo.com/manage/videos/706034606.

TACTICAL MEDIA MEETUP #2: SPECIAL SOLIDARITY SCREENINIG WITH KYIV BIENNIAL

MARIA VAN DER TOGT

TMR was proud to host a solidarity screening in collaboration with the Emergency Support Initiative by Kyiv Biennial and Home Cinema to raise funds for Ukraine. The event took the shape of a hybrid video broadcast, both physically screened and online broadcasted via homecinema.video, accompanied by a talk on media witnessing in times of crisis by Florian Göttke.

The screening featured a series of recent works by moving image artists based in Ukraine. All the works had been created in the two months following the Russian full-scale invasion; giving a raw and immediate insight into the filmmakers' practices. The works provided an intimate portrayal of individuals and groups caught up in bureaucracy and war. The films shown remind us of the importance of filmmaking in times of crisis and the necessity to make visible and archive traces as acts of resistance. They blatantly show the political dimensions of film and visual culture and the potential of artists' moving image practices as a medium of communicating, relating, and knowing.

The film selection was curated by Serge Klymko, who has been a practicing curator, cultural manager, researcher, and writer working on the intersection of visual and performative art, music, and urban ecosystems research in the last ten years. Over the past 5 years, he has curated a number of cultural and art projects in Barcelona, Geneva, Karlsruhe, Kyiv, Prague, Tbilisi, Vienna, and Warsaw, working with a wide range of artists and theoreticians. Serge is one of the organizers of Kyiv Biennial, an international forum for art, knowledge, and politics that integrates exhibitions and discussion platforms. From the beginning of the war, he founded ESI – Emergency Support Initiative, launched to help the Ukrainian artistic community under unprecedented conditions.[1]

HomeCinema is a video broadcasting platform for moving image works by young and emerging artists, created by Carmen Dusmet Carrasco and Andrea Gonzále.[2]

All proceeds from the screening went to the Emergency Support Initiative, launched to help the members of the artistic and cultural community in Ukraine who find themselves in need. The main goal of the fund is to offer support to people residing in the country and to provide them with immediate financial relief under the conditions of war, occupation and/or relocation.

---

1   Emergency Support Initiative. (2022). ESI. https://esi.kyivbiennial.org/en.
2   Home Cinema. (2022). Home Cinema. http://homecinema.video.

Screening Program

Alisa Sizykh
'15.02.22- 24.02.22 KYIV,' 2022

Daryna Snizhko
Another Night, 2022

Daria Molokoedova
Designers street, 2022

Petro Ryaska
Mask of White Snail, 2022

Liera Polianskova (SVITER art group)
How to Live During the Air Alarm, 2022

Taya Kabaeva
Untitled, 2022

Marichka Lukianchuk
Between Before and After, 2022

Eugene Arlov
The Budapest Gambit, 2022

Ania, resident of Mariupol
My house, My Yard and How We Lived Almost a Month, 2022

TACTICAL MEDIA MEETUP #3: DEBATE ON INTERNET BLOCKADE OF PROPAGANDIST MEDIA

11111 &23%#719

In the beginning of 2022, fake news still stood as an issue but was relegated to the background in comparison to the military-economic movements on the geopolitical plane. With the beginning of the war, the larger public discussion in Europe, from Italy to Germany and France has been focused primarily on the US and Europe's military support of Ukraine and its possible membership in the EU and NATO.

The same political levers of pressure and sanction are applied in parallel to the information war. Conspiracy theories and the concept of fake news are constantly being redefined in the context of the ongoing and highly mediated war in Ukraine. This intense dynamic, still straddling the lines of right-wing and left-wing discourse, provokes quick but not necessarily correct decisions on the part of political and media agents. This issue, however, the preconditions for which were observed before the war, has escalated since February and has explicitly divided the media community into two camps: the Internet Freedom supporters, who stand for the freedom of expression, and the Freedom of Press followers, who insist on propaganda censorship.

While the Netherlands hardly has an army to speak of, the IT or internet business and related infrastructure is considerable in size. During the turbulent 1990s, Press Now (the original name of Free Press Unlimited), the internet, and traditional media channels already came together (think of Zamir, B92, Vreme, etc). Thirty years ago, it was still a 'tactical' issue as both internet and store-forward bulletin board systems were still in their infancy.

Against the backdrop of the full-scale invasion of Ukraine, the Russian government has sharply increased funding for state media, resulting in an unprecedented level of state propaganda spread on social media platforms, causing an insurmountable flood of unverifiable digital content by the state-owned Russia Today and Sputnik on Instagram, Twitter, YouTube, and other social media on the conflict in Ukraine. Many US and EU lawmakers and Ukrainian officials have jolted into action by pressuring social media platforms attempting to curb Russian misinformation. So far, YouTube has said it would block *Russia Today* and *Sputnik* in the European Union, while Twitter and Meta, the parent of Facebook, have said they would label content from the outlets as state sponsored. In the EU, the decision to suspend the broadcasting activities of *Sputnik* and *Russia Today* was made in record time in March.

However, in the question of whether or not to censor *RT* and *Sputnik*, the two worlds of the internet and news media found themselves on opposite sides. The debate stems from a discussion between two important civilian parts of the work that is done in the Netherlands: within the new media culture, IT, and the internet world, and within the community that aims at supporting the independent press. A middle-of-the-road compromise is not readily conceivable in this case. It is about a hard choice that is on the table. Yet, does one support

Brussels's decision in this matter? Some will find the choice too blunt and will argue that internet freedom is not opposed to freedom of the press. Particularly, the blockade was criticized by the internet service providers, and internet freedom organizations for making a law precedent that can lead to the expansion of undemocratic censorship in Europe further: "allowing politicians to enact censorship policies overnight is wrong in principle" as well as it "could set a precedent for banning other politicized news outlets."[1] While some applaud the closing of Putin's propaganda channels, others see it as pointless and a prelude to much more far-reaching top-down regulation of the European internet. This seems to be a watershed moment for European legislation.

The third TMR meeting aims to address this important, albeit rather niche, issue, which has not been carried out across the board.

1   Sterling, T. (2022, May 25). *Dutch Journalists, Rights Group File Lawsuit Challenging EU Ban on RT, Sputnik*. Reuters. Retrieved July 10, 2022, from https://www.reuters.com/business/media-telecom/dutch-journalists-rights-group-file-lawsuit-challenging-eu-ban-rt-sputnik-2022-05-25/.

DEBATING THE EUROPEAN BLOCKADE OF RUSSIAN PROPAGANDIST MEDIA

MARIA PLICHTA

On June 30th, a debate on the European blockade of Russian propagandist media was organized by the Tactical Media Room at Spui25 in Amsterdam. After the beginning of the Russian full-scale invasion of Ukraine, the European Union banned *RT* and *Sputnik*, two prominent Russian state media outlets. The ban intends to limit the ability of the Russian state to wage an information war by weaponizing malicious propaganda. However, the move has been a divisive one—after all, isn't freedom of information central to the so-called 'European values'?

The event brought together a wide array of speakers, including academics, activists, and journalists. It opened with three short talks, by Ruben Brave, chairman of Internet Society Netherlands, Elmaz Asanova, a Crimean Tatar-Ukrainian journalist, and Sophia Kornienko, a Russian-Dutch journalist, whose statement was presented by moderator Chris Keulemans, in Sophia's absence. Ruben's opening talk focused on how cyberwarfare constituted a prelude to all-out war, pointing to Russia's attacks on Ukrainian internet infrastructure before the invasion began. Another key point made by Ruben is that propaganda tends to skillfully exploit existing societal issues, and without addressing those, vulnerability to disinformation remains inevitable.

Next, Elmaz sketched the grim landscape of practicing journalism under the Russian occupation of Crimea, which transformed her homeland into a "peninsula of fear and madness". She spoke of rampant discrimination of the indigenous Crimean Tatar population. Employing the tried-and-true tactic of labelling an opponent a dangerous extremist to justify ensuing repressions, the Tatars are denigrated as terrorists for their refusal to accept the occupation of their ancestral homeland. Elmaz ended her impassioned appeal by asking, "how long will I be humiliated in my native land?". Her full speech can also be read on page 72.

Kornienko's speech focused on a central tactic behind Russian propaganda: making people believe that there simply is no truth. By stripping the words of their original meaning, a delirious continuity is created between the past and present, in which "World War II never ends, fascists keep coming back", nothing really matters anymore, and even the greatest of crimes are justified. In Sophia's view, a powerful antidote to such manipulations is media literacy, and she emphasized the need to stop demonizing the internet as a place of lurking dangers, and to focus on its affordances for open communication instead.

After that, the discussion opened up to other panelists and audience members. The starting point was the question of whether freedom of speech is sacrosanct, or whether the distribution of content via the internet comes with responsibilities, and if so, where that responsibility lies. The first discussant to respond was Ilya Shcharbitski, a prominent Belarusian activist, who focused on the meaning of the notion of freedom in the post-Soviet space — or, as he defines it, the space of centuries-long Russification. He spoke of a prevalent lack of media literacy and suggested to try and address this problem by building independent media hubs in neighboring countries, as well as creating *samizdat* for the 21st century to counter the double propaganda (both domestic and Russian) in Belarus.

One of the central issues discussed was that of infrastructural neutrality. Niels ten Oever, a researcher of internet governance, mentioned three key premises in this context: that the internet is neither global, neutral or impartial but rather, embedded in an infrastructure of extraction and control built by multinational corporations. He called out the complicity of Western companies in actively building the infrastructure of surveillance employed by oppressive regimes. He stressed the need to reclaim the internet and its infrastructure, which would necessitate a radical rebuilding of ownership structures. A similar position was expressed by Leon Willems, who emphasized the need to hold big tech oligopolies responsible, tax them heavily, and redirect the resources towards independent journalism. If we want to reclaim the liberatory potential of communication, the infrastructure must be redesigned with that goal in mind.

Another perspective on infrastructural neutrality was expressed by Vesna Manojlovic, a senior community builder at RIPE NCC, the Regional Internet Registry for Europe and the Middle East. The organization's position is that "we can only be trusted as long as we remain neutral" and that disconnecting Russia can set a dangerous precedent for the curbing of information freedom. Manojlovic emphasized the importance of keeping connectivity open, regardless of what it might be used for, and expressed discomfort with going beyond the organization's administrative function to assume the role of a content-policing authoritative body.

The central reoccurring question of the debate was whether to block, or not to block? Both te Oever and Willems expressed their support for the idea of depriving state bodies of the ability to spread war-mongering propaganda. Te Oever emphasized that institutions do not fall under the purview of human rights, and therefore when the military actively violates these rights, it is fair game that their internet resources be suspended. A Russian member of the audience compared the state's propaganda to poisonous food. He argued that if information provides sustenance for the mind, toxic content can rightfully be put out of circulation. After all, as he said, back in the day uranium-laced ice cream used to exist, yet we would not argue that the freedom to sell it remains an inviolable human right.

Still, other speakers expressed their reservations about the efficacy of blocking as a solution. Another audience member, Dimitri, who had previously worked for Russian state media, expressed discomfort at the idea of fighting censorship with censorship, noting that cutting down on freedom of speech plays neatly into Putin's hands. Another argument against blocking access is rooted in the practical impossibility of effectively cleansing the internet of undesirable content; there are always channels through which to share it, and paradoxically, the attempt to get rid of it only serves to increase the appeal of such banned discourses.

What could be viable solutions to this double bind? One is to focus on increasing media literacy, a strategy favored by Kornienko and Brave, who emphasized the individual agency and responsibility inherent to sharing content online. This, however, is a contentious idea, which has been criticized as symptomatic of the neoliberal mindset which offloads responsibility for structural issues on individuals. To further complicate the issue, it is worth paying attention to a question raised by an audience member, Kristina Petrasova: are we even asking the right question by focusing on the issue of whether to ban or not? She made a strong appeal to redirect our attention to strengthening the ties to civil society, activists, and independent media in Russia, building solidarity instead of blockades.

A few concluding takeaways from this elaborate and nuanced debate might be that there is a pressing need to build stronger communicative bonds between communities, reclaim the technologies we have at our disposal so that they can better serve this goal, and keep resisting—both the propaganda of the Russian state and the neoliberal system that profits off proliferating such toxic discourses.

KEEP UKRAINE CONNECTED: INTERVIEW WITH THE CAMPAIGNERS

GEERT LOVINK

Mariupol went offline the minute the last 5G transmitter was destroyed. As soon as I heard about the Keep Ukraine Connected initiative,[1] I became curious about their activities. How do internet techies initiate a campaign to support Ukrainian internet service providers with hardware? Keep Ukraine Connected has been organized by the Global NOG Alliance.[2] NOG stands for Network Operator Group. In these groups, of which there is usually one per country, network engineers exchange information about their work. NOGs have existed since the early days of the internet and the members also have a certain influence on the further development of internet protocols and techniques. The Global NOG Alliance is an association of friends from the industry dedicated to helping NOGs around the world. Now they are helping Ukrainian Network Operators keep the internet running through the war by fundraising and collecting and distributing equipment. As René Fichtmüller explained to the German magazine *Zeit Online*, the highest priority is so-called splicing equipment. This makes it possible to re-join severed fibre optic cables that have been cut, for example, by a bomb. But generators are also always important, because without electricity, servers and switches cannot be operated and consequently there is no internet. "Ukraine was and is a highly networked country and internet access," René Fichtmüller explains. "For example, Ukraine was one of the world's leading countries in smartphone payments and social media is extremely important for young people, even, or especially, in times of war. For all this to work, the fibre-optic and mobile networks must be intact. But the experts on the ground lack the material." For instance, with enough generators it is possible to bring villages or individual businesses back online.

Fichtmüller also told a Czech news website that stolen graphics cards from computers in corporate offices and datacenters are currently being traded.[3] "I've also seen photos indicating that some providers have to deal with destroyed PoPs (Points of Presence), both in metropolitan and long-distance networks. Satellite connectivity via Starlink can be a good backup, but this can also be a risk, as the satellite signal can be misused to locate the receiver, which can then become the target of an attack."

I had a short email exchange with Sander Steffann (based in Apeldoorn/NL), who, at some point, also joined the Tactical Media Room. With the help of others, he was so kind as to answer questions.

1   Pritchard, C. (2022, June 28). *Keep Ukraine Connected*. Global NOG Alliance. https://nogalliance.org/our-task-forces/keep-ukraine-connected/.
2   Pritchard, C. (2022a, May 25). *About us*. Global NOG Alliance. https://nogalliance.org.
3   Slížek, D. (2022, April 12). *Keep Ukraine Connected: Jak pomoc ukrajinským poskytovatelům internetu putovala i z Česka*. Lupa.cz. https://www.lupa.cz/clanky/keep-ukraine-connected-jak-pomoc-ukrajinskym-poskytovatelum-internetu-putovala-i-z-ceska/.

Geert Lovink: Can you tell us about your Ukrainian partners? Where are they located and what are the challenges they are confronted with? What kind of damage are they dealing with?

Sander Steffann: We are working mainly with the Ukrainian Internet Association (the Network Operators Group), the Association of Rights Holders and Content Providers (a broader Telecoms organisation), and a company called DEPS, based in Lviv, who are handling distribution of the equipment we're providing. Since the war they have pivoted from reselling equipment to distributing it to Network Operators in need all over Ukraine. They don't charge us, or the people the equipment is distributed to. We have also had some support from the Ministry for Digital Transformation—they've been instrumental in helping us get the paperwork right for the border crossing.

GL: Can you give us an update where the Keep Ukraine Campaign stands at the moment? We're now four months into the invasion.

SS: We're very proud of the network of volunteers that's building up around the campaign. In particular our volunteer drivers, who are doing a brilliant job of ferrying equipment over the border. We still have some significant challenges. We potentially have several hundred pallets of equipment in our database—some of which are coming from outside the EU. We need useful and flexible short and long term storage solutions: While some of the equipment is in high demand and can be shipped quickly, we expect a lot of it will be of more use during the reconstruction phase. Most logistics companies work on the basis of high product flow, so it's been difficult for us to find suitable spaces. We are also trying to navigate the maze that is customs and borders so we can get better at receiving donations as well as delivering them. In particular we are seeking contacts in the Polish government who can help us by providing safe, speedy passage for our drivers at border crossings. We are also looking for expertise in Customs and Taxes so that we can spend the money we've raised more efficiently.

GL: John Gilmore once said: "The Net interprets censorship as damage and routes around it." One can also interpret this statement as as a call to ignore the damage caused by inner-European conflicts over ancient borders of competing empires. Why take sides, perhaps instead continue business as usual? The internet as such doesn't need Ukraine. Maybe the other way round, yes...

SS: Our chair Rene Fichtmuller says it best: "Our Tech Community is one big family. We don't think in colors, we don't think in races or genders, we don't think in borders." Unlike big operators, who are free to choose the profit motive if they wish, our aim is to help people learn about and benefit from access to the internet. Right now the people in need of help are in Ukraine. Tomorrow, it could be a tsunami in Bangladesh, an epidemic in Haiti, or some other conflict that has destroyed connectivity somewhere in the world. We hope to take what we learn from our Keep Ukraine Connected Taskforce and apply that knowledge wherever it is needed. The internet is now an integral part of all our lives. The connectivity it provides deserves to be protected.

GL: Do you believe internet engineers should listen to directives from Brussels to ban Putin's propaganda television channels on the Web such as *RT* and *Sputnik*?

SS: As individuals we are all free to live by our own conscience. Since we are working closely with the Association of Rights and Content Providers—which includes television channel operators—we have discussed this in depth with our Ukrainian colleagues. The conclusion we came to is that instead of banning the Russian propaganda outlets—a staple of Ukrainian television for much of the population since long before the war—we would instead support the connectivity of Ukraine-based channels that the Russian forces have been working hard to bring down, and promote alternative ways of getting to those channels wherever relevant. Removing misinformation from the internet is a Sisyphean task—you can keep rolling that rock up the hill all you like—it's just going to roll back down again. Better to give people access to more reliable sources of information instead.

PRESENTING UNE (THE UNIVERSITY OF NEW EUROPE) & ITS MENTOR PROGRAMME

ELLEN RUTTEN

In this text I introduce two initiatives by a collective of scholars and activists from across Europe in response to the Russian war in Ukraine:[1]

*   A plan for the University of New Europe (UNE) – a new university with ample space for scholars, students, and cultural workers at risk from, firstly, Ukraine and, secondly, Belarus and Russia; and

*   A spin-off of this project – the Akno/UNE mentor programme, which targets the same groups of students and colleagues.

In my role as Professor of Slavic studies at the University of Amsterdam, I have been a part of both initiatives from the start – but both are collective projects, which would be unthinkable without the efforts of colleagues, students, and institutions whom I introduce in some more detail below.

UNE

UNE – the University of New Europe – is an initiative that historian Alexander Etkind (Central European University, Vienna) and Jan Claas Behrends (WZB Berlin Social Science Center/Viadrina European University Frankfurt) founded in June 2021. Frustrated by protest repressions in Belarus and Russia, Etkind, Behrends and I wrote an open letter to the EU and its member states, in which we plead for more porous borders and humanitarian visas for critical thinkers from Belarus and Russia; plus for a new university in response to the acute risk that an increasing number of critical Russians and Belarusians were facing. We ended the letter with the following call for action:

> Relying on the successful experience of such transnational institutions of higher learning as the European University Institute, Central European University, the European University Viadrina Frankfurt, the European Humanities University, College of Europe, and CIVICA (an alliance of eight European universities in social sciences), we need to create a new East European University located in one of the member-states of the EU. We ... welcome public and private initiatives aimed at funding and hosting such an institution of higher education. It will provide new opportunities for those who were fired, repressed and forced to leave their homes, and also for those who wish to learn and study according to high European standards. We will commit our intellectual resources, experience, and leadership to creating such a university.[2]

---

1   I thank Maria-Laetizia von Bibra for assisting me in finalizing this text.
2   "Open letter: we need a new university for eastern Europe," June 2021, *https://www.opendemocracy. net/en/odr/open-letter-we-need-new-university-eastern-europe/*.

The letter was signed by fifty high-profile scholars and thinkers, including world-renowned philosophers (such as Judith Butler and Slavoj Žižek), cultural and media theorists (such as Mieke Bal, Marianne Hirsch, Boris Groys and Geert Lovink), journalists (such as Masha Gessen and Zhanna Nemtsova), and writers (such as Dmitry Bykov, Lev Rubinstein, and Nobel Prize Winner Olga Tokarczuk), among others. We published translations of this letter across different European media, including Dutch newspaper *de Volkskrant*, the *Frankfurter Allgemeine Zeitung*, *Corriere della Sera*, and Swedish *Morgenbladet*.

Our open letter marked the launch of the University of New Europe. Since the autumn of 2021, an international steering group of seven scholars and activists from Western and Eastern Europe has been actively lobbying for the creation of this institution. As a group, we assert that Europe – not Eastern Europe, but Europe as a whole – is confronting new challenges, which are not limited to but include:

A new war in the heart of Europe
Climate crisis and environmental degradation
Migration and humanitarian crises
Expanding and sophisticated authoritarianism
The enormous complexity of the post-pandemic Green Deal[3]

We are convinced that in response to these crisises, we need a new educational and scholarly space for shared learning, research and dialogue – one that "provides the soft power necessary to explore and respond to these challenges."[4] With this aim in mind, the new institution needs teaching programs in which academics, artists, journalists, activists, artists, designers and NGO representatives cooperate actively, and in which the need to address pressing societal challenges is built in from the start. Of course existing universities – particularly those transnational spaces of higher education that we mentioned in our open letter – also actively address these challenges. But even when taken as a whole, Europe's existing higher education system simply cannot harbor the vast amounts of critical students, academics, and cultural workers who are currently in need of new homes, and new places to think freely.

In our open letter, we called for an 'East European University' – but with time, we moved away from the idea of an exclusively Eastern-European institution towards a vision of a more transnational shared space of learning, research and dialogue. Within this space, we will welcome students and staff members from across different world localities. But in view of recent illiberalization developments, we do believe that the new institution needs to allocate a substantial number of places – say, fifty to sixty percent – to scholars, students, and cultural workers who are at risk. Firstly, this group includes Ukrainian colleagues and students, whom the Russian war in Ukraine has placed in acute or life-threatening danger, and who should currently be prioritized when filling at-risk positions. Secondly, we will create positions for Belarusian and Russian colleagues and students who now face the risk of persecution for

3   The citation comes from our website, *https://neweurope.university*.
4   Ibid.

political reasons. Last but far from least, we plan to allocate part of the at-risk positions to students and staff from outside Europe. With this last step, we offer at least a modest response to the current dearth of options for this large and underprioritized group of colleagues and students in need; but it also helps to prevent the creation of a Eurocentric institution and to amplify inclusive, globally oriented spaces for knowledge-building.

The war has ramped up the logistic pace of our work on UNE. Our steering group is currently conducting conversations about six draft MA programs with colleagues from Latvia, where the initiative has active support from the mayor of Riga, multiple Latvian parliamentarians, and the Minister of Foreign Affairs. At the same time, UNE is a university in the making – and making a university is no quick-and-dirty task. There are several, particularly financial, hurdles to be overcome before we can speak of an actual Latvian or other physical institution. At the moment, we are patiently tackling those hurdles one by one, with support from the German Slavic Association, the Akademische Netzwerk Osteuropa, the Dutch Young Academy, the Netherlands Institute of Advanced Studies, the University of Amsterdam, and the Institute of Network Cultures, among a broader and steadily growing range of institutions and individuals who have gracefully agreed to help us in realizing our plans.

The UNE mentor program

The University of New Europe, in short, is a long-term project. An ambitious – some would say megalomaniac – plan like this cannot be realized without cautious long-term logistic planning and detailed work on ethical and moral challenges. How, for one, does one responsibly unite Ukrainian and Russian students and scholars around the same table, at a time when more than one expert voice claims that this is impossible in times of war? This process takes time – and when the Russian war in Ukraine reached a new gear in February 2022, we were increasingly worried that we could not offer instant support at a time that which support is needed so urgently. The UNE team then decided that, alongside our work on a physical institution, we also needed to create shorter-term solutions to provide emergency support, and to focus at least part of attention on making it easier for people to find and make use of existing opportunities. With this aim in mind, we created the so-called Akno/UNE mentoring programme, in partnership with Akno, a German Eastern-Europe association that safeguards academic freedom.[5]

The Akno/UNE mentor programme connects at-risk students, scholars, cultural workers, and artists from, most importantly, Ukraine, as well as from Belarus and Russia to experienced professionals from elsewhere. With this programme, we try to act as matchmakers between these two groups and to offer personal mentors to at-risk students and colleagues. In our introductory message, we provide each mentor/mentee pair with a link to our resource list – an interactive survey of available options for the purposes of fleeing, emergency relief, shelter, or fellowships.[6]

---

5   *https://akno.network/*.
6   Resources for Academics and Cultural Workers at Risk (crowdsourced and updated daily): *https://neweurope.university/wp-content/uploads/2022/06/UNE-Emergency-Contacts-and-Funding_28-June-2022.pdf*.

The idea behind the Akno/UNE mentor programme is simple. Mentors are asked to schedule a series of online meetings with their mentees. Ideally, at the first meeting, mentees share their concerns and wishes or needs; the mentors then use the resource list, their network connections, and/or their skills with grant or application writing to help formulate the best scenario for their mentee. This *can* mean jointly concluding that there are no options at the moment – in which case the mentor connection can still be a useful lifeline or form of moral support. It can also mean jointly discussing and exploring options to relocate, or exploring remote support options (these options are important for Ukrainian academics or cultural workers, many of whom want to continue their work without leaving Ukraine).

In addition to the resource list, we offer regular mentor/mentee consult hours to advise participants on the process of mentorship. At an upcoming consult hour, a certified psychologist has been asked to share some relevant links and advice, for instance.

Together with the Leiden-based slavist and cultural historian Dorine Schellens and a team of nine assistants and volunteers,[7] we have currently paired about 450 people in the programme (225 mentees and 225 mentors). A small-scale evaluation showed us that the mentor connection has made a tangible positive difference to the professional futures of several mentees. At the same time, we are encountering various obstacles, ranging from a lack of academic options available for scholars from Russia and Ukraine to failures of communication between mentors and mentees (where those occur, we offer mentees a new connection).

We welcome new mentees – and those who are reading this who have experience with grant writing and who want to support a colleague or student in need, are also welcome to visit our site and register as a mentor.[8] If you choose to join our mentor project, we thank you in advance for your costly time and efforts. Please also keep an eye out for news about the University of New Europe. We hope to soon start attracting donations, and the new institution can use all the help and support that committed professionals are willing to offer.

---

7   Special thanks go to Maria-Laetizia von Bibra, Julie Haverd, Kirstine Arentoft Kristensen, Mari Janssen, and Margarita Shaburova for their work on the Akno/UNE mentor programme
8   *https://neweurope.university*; for historical context, also see *https://overdemuur.org/de-oorlog-in-oekraine-als-kenniscrisis-hoe-kunnen-we-steun-en-solidariteit-bieden-aan-academische-gemeenschappen-in-nood/* (in Dutch).

INFORMATIONAL EXPORT

TIME IS DEAD AND MEANING HAS NO MEANING

SOPHIA KORNIENKO

This party never stops, time is dead and meaning has no meaning. Existence is upside down and I reign supreme.

My daughter loves reciting whole dialogues from Disney's animated series Gravity Falls, but this particular quote, by the show's demonic antagonist, has really stuck with me as a prophetic description of our post-postmodern time: *"This party never stops, time is dead and meaning has no meaning".*

I remember how back in early 2014, I was a guest on Dutch television arguing that King William Alexander and Princess Maxima shouldn't go to Russia and drink champagne with Putin. It was just a few weeks prior to the Russian invasion of the Crimea. The host asked me something along the lines of *"Why should we be careful with Putin, what danger, what threat does he pose to the West?"* to which I answered *"Russia's main export is not oil and gas, but the idea that there is no truth."*

Year after year, the Kremlin has been pouring hundreds of millions of dollars into this particular export. Putin has signed a decree forbidding budget cuts in this area and gave out military awards to the heads of the media corporations producing brain fog.

Whether it was Russia's grey cardinal, Putin's former advisor and postmodernist writer Vladislav Surkov's idea or one of Putin's own psychological manipulation strategies, there was a point in Russian foreign politics when this whole post-postmodern surrealist tactic that nothing is what it seems, everybody lies, or everybody has their own truth, started spilling abroad.

It wasn't about censorship, it was about deflating once meaningful words such as 'war' or 'nazi' to empty sounds. It wasn't about keeping secrets but about creating so many wild and vastly different versions of every event in what was already a very informationally saturated environment, that the audience would start thinking the truth was unknowable. It wasn't about expressing an opposing view but about attacking what is called "capillarity" or organic, meaningful interconnectedness and organic discussion on the web by fabricating swarms of fake identities at troll farms that would break up meaningful connections and make discussion futile.

The Oxford Internet Institute which studies state-controlled media, published a report in 2020 stating that one of *RT*'s objectives was to encourage conspiracy theories about media institutions in the West in order to discredit and delegitimize them.[1]

---

1   M Elswah, M., & Howard, P. N. (2020). "Anything that Causes Chaos": The Organizational Behavior of
     Russia Today (RT). Journal of Communication, 70(5), 623–645. https://doi.org/10.1093/joc/jqaa027.

Of course, this gaping abyss between image and meaning is hardly Putin's invention. Jean Baudrillard's theory of empty simulacra has become a classic in media studies, exacerbated by digital technologies.

Back in 2006, I wrote my MA thesis at the Media department of the University of Amsterdam about how the image of Islam in the media has lost its meaning. I must apologize for the graphic allusion, but sinister performances of the terror attacks in the early 2000s were like a postmodern reenactment of René Magritte, especially Golconda, depicting well-off men in suits suspended in mid-air. Everything was for the show, for the horrific theatrical effect. The political leaders behind fundamentalist suicide teams manufactured their own simulacra of Islamic ideology and disinformation not because they believed in it, but because it was their strategy and it produced a terrifying effect.

Kremlin is doing something very similar, but taking it a whole lot further: *Ceci n'est pas une pomme/pipe.* "This is not war", "This is not pregnant women being shelled", "This is not a trade center being targeted", it says, waging a bloody war and targeting civilians in open daylight, its main goal to spread terror. Writer Vladimir Sorokin has even suggested Putin may not be hoping for a victory, but doing everything purely for the horrific effect, for media, and for historic attention.[2] Like a suicide terrorist. And Russian film director Sergei Loznitsa has observed how in reaction to hopeless, desperate life situations humans rely on surrealism as a coping mechanism.[3]

In November 2021, Surkov penned yet another essay, openly stating that Russia should be pushing its tension and "social entropy" (read: export terror and chaos) across its borders, relieving itself in a weird expression of the second law of thermodynamics.

It is in this uncertainty (that is, of course, not only created by the orchestrated disinformation campaigns but by the very fast pace of change in the world today) that even in the democratic world, many people are extremely gullible to conspiracy theories and manipulation, because it helps them to at least find simple explanations/culprits responsible for their misfortunes in the otherwise chaotic sea of information.

In the 'Gravity Falls' animated series, the diabolic antagonist says he liberates the world this way, by stripping it of meaning. Indeed, if facts no longer matter, if the borderline between war and peace is smudged, there is no grip, no future. Time is dead. WW2 never ends, fascists keep coming back. Anything you do doesn't matter anymore. Any crime. Any mass murder.

So what should be our coping mechanisms in the face of this, as disinformation researcher Peter Pomerantsev put it, postmodern politics of "radical relativism"?[4]

2 Chazan, G. (2022, June 24). Writer Vladimir Sorokin: 'I underestimated the power of Putin's madness.' *Financial Times*. https://www.ft.com/content/1f4bd315-7753-4e7a-be4e-0ea7e31522b9.
3 Peter Pomerantsev, This Is Not Propaganda: Adventures in the War Against Reality. Faber & Faber, 2019. https://www.ft.com/content/1f4bd315-7753-4e7a-be4e-0ea7e31522b9.
4 A Applebaum, A., & Pomerantsev, P. (2022, February 16). How to Put Out Democracy's Dumpster Fire. *The Atlantic*. https://www.theatlantic.com/magazine/archive/2021/04/the-internet-doesnt-have-to-be-awful/618079/.

I was quite taken aback upon hearing that a few of my European colleagues from the Freedom of Information Coalition have launched a complaint about the legitimacy of the EU-wide blockade of Russian state channels, such as *RT* and *Sputnik*, "calling the proportionality of the measure into question". In May 2022, they signed a "petition that seeks to preserve access to all information" and sent it to the European Court in Luxembourg.

At a time when every-day political decisions about military support of Ukraine literally decide not only the fate of Ukraine but of Europe and the West, entities that still have meaning, albeit fragile,such as European NGOs spend their resources on trying to help the Kremlin's main instruments of manipulation back into the EU and hence empower them to influence those political decisions.

Cybersecurity experts define two main components of cybersecurity. Protection from coordinated disinformation and harassment campaigns is number one. One must add, especially at a time of unprecedented aggression.

Number two is putting internet users in charge of their private data, to make sure that the likes of Cambridge Analytica never get hold of it. Perhaps something that can't be achieved as urgently but is being very actively talked about now, in terms of self-sovereign identity: DIDs (decentralized identifiers) and decentralized networks, technologies that should enable all of us to store our data in our own wallets and nodes instead of on social media accounts.

The same technology will make it very easy to verify social media accounts as *genuine,* as opposed to automated bots or fake identities.

Independent researchers are also busy developing verification AIs, as well as strategies to train social media algorithms and to hold tech giants accountable.

A recent MIT Medialab study published in *Nature* found that "the current design of social media platforms—in which users scroll quickly through a mixture of serious news and emotionally engaging content, and receive instantaneous quantified social feedback on their sharing—may discourage people from reflecting on accuracy". The researchers suggest "interventions that social media platforms could use to increase users' focus on accuracy. For example, platforms could periodically ask users to rate the accuracy of randomly selected headlines, simultaneously generating useful crowd ratings that can help to identify misinformation. Such an approach could (in the long run) potentially increase the quality of news circulating online without relying on a centralized institution to certify truth and censor falsehood[5]".

---

5   Pen Pennycook, G., Epstein, Z., Mosleh, M., Archer, A. A., Eckles, D., & Rand, D. G. (2021). Shifting attention to accuracy can reduce misinformation online. *Nature*, 590–595. https://doi.org/10.1038/s41586-021-03344-2.

Yet, the most powerful antidote to manipulation in the free world is media literacy. This is why we should stop enforcing the stereotype of the web as a dark, dangerous place and instead see it as a tool for digital democracy, meaningful connections, and knowledge. The algorithms reinforce what we make of it.

While collecting signatures in support of independent Russian journalists and having (with the help of my children) built a Discord server for these journalists, I was shocked at the low levels of tech literacy among my colleagues.

It is essential that kids and teens, currently subject to inhumane ageist discrimination and screen control culture, imposed by regulators who lag years behind in their understanding of technological processes, get better access to the web and the emerging metaverse. It is those who have been highly regulated and have been unable to teach themselves basic media literacy that easily fall prey to manipulators.

Those who have only been allowed a couple of hours per day online, exhausted, are used to regarding this time online as their unwind time of meaningless scrolling. Let's enable a new generation of meaningful creators, respected in their right to get all the time they need to get to the bottom of things in the world's pool of knowledge. Let's be there for them to hear them out, instead of controlling them.

THE PRECIPICE – UKRAINE'S INTER-WHITE WAR IS JUST THE BEGINNING: WELCOME TO THE GEOPOLITICS OF CHAOS

FRANCO 'BIFO' BERARDI

The text was originally published in Italian on NOT (April 12th, 2022). The English version was then republished on the INC website (April 15th, 2022), translated by Tommaso Campagna and Laurence Scherz. Here, the text is republished with the author's consent.

> This is not the time of Your judgment, Francis punctuated, addressing God from the empty Square on Easter night 2020, but of our judgment: the time to choose what matter and what passes away, the time to separate what is necessary from what is not.
> *(Marco Politi, Francesco, la peste, la rinascita)*

The internal enemy

The logic of war is horror.

In the semiotic of war, all horror news, even fake news, is effective because they produce hatred and fear. Why be outraged if the U.S. drops phosphorus bombs on Fallujah or the Russians kill unarmed prisoners in Bucha? Are we talking about war crimes? But war is a crime in itself, an automatic chain of crimes.

The question that needs to be answered is: who is responsible for this war? Who wanted, provoked, armed, and unleashed it?

Russian Nazi-Stalinism led by Putin, no doubt about it. But everyone can see that someone else strongly wanted this war and is actively feeding it.

If in February the European Union had convened an international conference to discuss Lavrov's requests, the war machine could have been stopped. Instead, it was preferred to fan the flames. A Ukrainian delegate participating in the talks with the Russians candidly stated, 'I am surprised. Why did NATO declare so early on that in case of war it would not intervene? In doing so, it invited Russia to escalate.'[1]

Those who participate in war are unable to think. For neuro-cognitive reasons that are fairly easy to understand, those who wage war have no time to think, they must save their lives, they must kill those who might make an attempt on their lives.

---

1   Limes, R. (2022, April 15). *L'ultima parola ai popoli muti*. Limes. https://www.limesonline.com/cartaceo/lultima-parola-ai-popoli-muti.

And they must first silence the internal enemy.

The internal enemy is the sensitivity of being human: the conscience if you will. Freud talks about it in a text on war neuroses, written during the First World War: the internal enemy manifests itself as doubt, hesitation, fear, desertion. The internal enemy is the will to think.

Here, today, the entire media and political system is intent on defeating the internal enemy: Federico Rampini accuses the director of L'Avvenire of working for Putin, and the Pope's words are censored by the entire Italian media system, and Francesco Merlo invites to linch the undecided.[2]

We are already far ahead in the process of militarization of the public discourse and the Italian political and journalistic class is obediently entering the brain into a nationalist cluster. In that cluster it becomes difficult to distinguish the voices of extreme right journalists and those of intellectuals with a Trotskyist or Lotta Continua background.

The media system has undergone a striking mutation in the past two years. During the pandemic, it was constantly mobilized for health purposes. Twenty-four hours a day, we were shown ambulances, green aprons, ventilation equipment, and from a certain point moment on injections, syringes, and more injections and more syringes, in an anxiety-inducing and intimidating, uninterrupted stream. Someone predicted that this health media siege was the preamble to a definitive media mutation. Now for twenty-four hours a day, we see terrifying spectacles, mutilated bodies, the desperate and painful flight of mothers and children. For twenty-four hours a day, we witness the vociferous crowding of commentators, of pundits, of generals calling for war, and silencing the internal enemy.

What I would do if I lived in Kiev

I too wondered: what would I do if I lived in Kiev? For days this question tormented me. My father participated in the Italian Resistance against fascism, I said to myself; so wouldn't it be my duty to support the resistance of the Ukrainian people? Shouldn't I fight for the values that Russian aggression puts in danger?

Then I remembered that my father was not an anti-fascist when he had to escape from the barracks in Padua where he was a private. He had never considered the problem, fascism was an obvious natural condition for him, as it was for the vast majority of Italians. When the Italian army melted after September 8th, he escaped like many others, he went to visit his family in Bologna but his parents had fled the city because they feared the bombings. So, with his brother, he decided to flee to the Marche region, who knows why. They found a group of other evacuees, met some partisans and joined them. To defend his life he became a partisan. Talking with the partisans it seemed to him that the most prepared and generous

---

2 L. (2022, March 30). *LA7*. La7.it. https://www.la7.it/laria-che-tira/video/federico-rampini-contro-marco-tarquinio-ignobile-mettere-sullo-stesso-piano-sanzioni-e-bombardamenti-30-03-2022-431755.

were communists, and he understood that the communists had an explanation for the past and a plan for the future: so he became a communist.

If I lived in Kiev and there was someone who explained to me that I had to defend the Free World, Democracy, the Values of the West, all words with a capital letter, I would defect. But maybe I would decide to join the resistance to defend my home, my brothers: all words with a lower case letter.

So I don't know how to answer the questions I ask myself: whether I would participate in the Ukrainian resistance, whether I would shoot Russian soldiers or not. What I do know for sure is that the capital reasons why the Free World calls Ukrainians to resistance are false. And false is the rhetoric of the Europeans inciting to continue the show.

Nazism is an evolution of humiliation

An orgy of horror is unleashed in Europe, as it has been unleashed for a couple of decades in Syria, Afghanistan, Iraq, Libya, Yemen. But those were distant places, inhabited by people different from us; or rather, to be precise: inhabited by people we hate and consider inferior.

Vladimir Putin, who never hid his imperial vocation and his Stalinist methods when our presidents, businessmen, and journalists courted him, started this war because the majority of the Russian people reacted to the humiliation of the last thirty years in the same way the Germans reacted to the humiliation of Versailles in the 1930s.

Nazism is an evolution of humiliation, it is a promise of aggressive redemption against humiliation. And anyone who wants to know the depth of humiliation suffered by Russians since the 1990s should read Svetlana Aleksievic's Secondhand Time.[3]

But, as the well-composed Xi says, 'a hand alone makes no noise.' Putin's hand is not enough. The other hand is that of Joe Biden, who pushed the Russians and Ukrainians to war so he could cash in on four results: politically destroy the European Union, prevent the construction of Nord Stream 2, rise in the electoral polls in his country, and defeat the Russian enemy.

The first two objectives have been achieved perfectly. The Nord Stream 2 project has been canceled by the German government, so now Europe has to get its supplies from the American market, where the fuel costs a bit more, and in any case, will not even be remotely enough to replace Russian gas.

Politically, the European Union has been subjected to the will of NATO and forced to identify itself as a nation, which is exactly the opposite of what the founders of the Union had intended.

The European Union was born to escape the nationalist obsession of the twentieth century,

---

3   Alexievich, S., & Shayevich, B. (2019). *Second-Hand Time*. Fitzcarraldo Editions.

but in early 2022 NATO turned it into a nation. And now the Europe-Nation is going to the baptism of fire of war like any self-respecting nation.

As for the other two results, the matter is more complicated, because 55% of Americans disapprove of Biden's foreign policy (it never happened before, not even in the days of Vietnam, not even in the days of Iraq, that the majority disapproves of the President's war). Electoral preferences, according to polls, are not positive: Biden has climbed back up from 36% to 44%, but that's not enough. It is likely that the Democrats will lose the November election, and later a Republican (we'll see which one, but I wouldn't rule out Donald Trump) will win the presidential election.

As for the last result that Biden wanted to achieve, the defeat of Russia, things are even more complicated. Despite the fierce resistance of the Ukrainian people, Russia is achieving what it set out to do, namely the destruction of the Ukrainian military apparatus, and control over the southeastern territories and Crimea. Russian soldiers die by the thousands and even Russian generals fall during the fighting, a fact Putin cares less than zero about. Sacrifice is the soul of Russian nationalist mystique, as anyone who has read Tolstoy, Isaak Babel and Aleksandr Blok knows.

Thereafter, it is foreseeable that the conflict will become endemic on Ukrainian territory and Russia will enter a phase of economic and social catastrophe. In this case, however, we must be aware that an internal war in a country with 6,000 nuclear warheads is bearing some unprecedented risks.

Life is a paradise

According to some polls, 83% of Russians support the war.[4] I don't believe it, I think the polls coming from Moscow are not reliable. But it is likely that aggression enjoys majority support.

A growing minority of young Russians is also turning to the ideas of the ultra-nationalists for whom the war in Ukraine is a self-purification of the Russian soul as a prelude to broader adventures. 'Thanks to you, Ukraine, who taught us to be Russians again!' declares in lyrical tones an idiot named Ivan Okhlobystin.[5]

There is a long tradition of martyrology that descends from orthodox spiritualism, that passes through Dostojevski, and crosses the twentieth century, reappearing in Vasily Grossman and in Aleksandr Solzenicyn himself. This mystical victimhood is summed up in the words of the dying brother of the monk Zosima in The Brothers Karamazov: 'Mother, do not weep, life is a paradise, and we are all in paradise, but we do not want to recognize it, for if we had the will to recognize it, tomorrow paradise would be established throughout the entire world.'

---

4   Tg24, R. S. (2022, April 6). *Guerra Ucraina, sondaggio: "83% dei russi sostiene Putin."* Sky. https://tg24. sky.it/mondo/2022/04/06/guerra-ucraina-putin-sondaggi-russia.
5   *Ivan Okhlobystin. Monologue: "Thank you, Ukraine!"* (2018, June 8). Top War. https://en.topwar. ru/53714-ivan-ohlobystin-monolog-spasibo-tebe-ukraina.html.

The paradise Dostojevski talks about is pain, cold, misery, torture, in short: the cross. Russian Orthodox nationalism loves pain as proof of closeness to Christ on the cross, and loves the people as much as it hates concrete women and men: 'How repugnant men are,' says Raskol'nikov before committing the senseless crime that precisely because of its senselessness must be carried out.

American ignorance is faced with Russian delirium and it is not an easy encounter. Americans (I am of course speaking of the class that holds political and media power in that country) have never been able to understand cultural differences, except as backwardness and inferiority to be exploited, subjugated, or corrected by slaps. But the Russian cultural difference remains, irreducible in its mixture of redeeming universalism and a cult of suffering that is both endured and inflicted.

Russian madness and American ignorance have dragged Europe into a precipice, from which, by now, it seems difficult to slow down.

The leading country in the Free World

In the country that leads the Free World (with a capital letter, mind you), police routinely kill three people a day, usually black.

In 2020, after the Black Lives Matter uprising when it came to getting the black and the left vote, the American Democratic Party pledged to reduce funding for police and to invest heavily in improving social conditions. Of course, these promises were not kept: no cancellation of student debt and so on. But especially no reduction in funding for the police. On the contrary, funding increases.

At the Mexican border, the rejection of migrants has reached levels that will make one regret the days of Donald Trump (which will soon return, however).

For one reason or another, support for Biden fell to its lowest levels. After August in Kabul, Biden had to prove that even though America had lost the war against the world's shakiest country, it could win it against Russia. So he couldn't consider the repeated requests of Sergei Lavrov, who constantly repeated that Russia wanted to discuss its security, its borders, and thus the expansion that NATO has pursued for the last twenty-five years.

As old men who rebel against their own painful impotence often do, Biden decided to confront the Russians head-on, preparing for high noon with Putin. But when it came time to pull out the gun, the Ukrainians were left alone in front of the Kremlin's Stalin-Tsarist criminal.

Euro-American sponsors of the Ukrainian resistance have provided weapons and media support. But it is Ukrainians who are dying, whose long history of oppression has, understandably, pushed them toward ultra-nationalist positions.

An inter-white war precipitates the new geopolitics of chaos

Besides the psychopathology of senile dementia,[6] which plays an essential role in the psychotic collapse of the white (Russian-European-American) race, what is the strategic motivation of this war? Biden is categorical: it is necessary to defend the free world, meaning the West, of which he has decided to be leader again. Defending the West after five centuries of colonization, violence, systematic robbery and racism has become difficult. As we will soon see, the Russian-American choice to go to inter-white war has precipitated white decline, turning it into collapse.

What began on February 24 is an inter-white war, where the white race fights against the white race: but from this war will emerge — or indeed is already emerging — new post-global geopolitics.

When in 1989 the free world defeated the socialist sphere, opening the way to the privatization of the world and to the financial imposition of neoliberalism, ideologists wondered if this new order was irrevocable and eternal, and therefore if history was over, with all its conflicts, revolts and wars. Francis Fukuyama pronounced a bit hastily in this sense, and liberal-democrats strutted: democracy and market were an unbeatable pair.[7]

Coupled with the iron law of the market, the word democracy soon revealed itself to be meaningless: every four or five years, the citizens of the free world could choose their representatives; but their representatives could do no more than apply the laws of the market, whose automatic logic could not be undermined by political will.

This scam could not last, and from 2016 on, democracy is reduced to a joke.

Someone, a little less dumb than Fukuyama, wrote a book to explain that an era of conflict between civilizations had begun. In The Clash of Civilizations and the Remaking of the World Order Samuel Huntington described in broad terms the geopolitics of this clash, which in his opinion, should have opposed a number (seven, perhaps, more or less) of civilizational blocs against each other.[8]

In some ways, Huntington's theory described identity (ethnic, religious, cultural) as the dividing line between conflicting forces, and it anticipated the American wars against Islamic countries, and the coming clash between the West and the Chinese world. Huntington was not as dramatically wrong as Fukuyama, but his theory trivializes a much more complex process.

6   *War and (Senile) Dementia - Journal #125 March 2022 - e-flux.* (2022, March). E-Flux. https://www.e-flux.com/journal/125/454088/war-and-senile-dementia/.
    Guerra & demenza (senile) | Not | NERO. (2022, February 28). Not. https://not.neroeditions.com/guerra-demenza-senile/.
7   *La fine della storia e l'ultimo uomo.* (2022, July 6). Utet Libri. https://www.utetlibri.it/libri/la-fine-della-storia-e-lultimo-uomo/.
8   contributori di Wikipedia. (2021, July 22). *Lo scontro delle civiltà.* Wikipedia. https://it.wikipedia.org/wiki/Lo_scontro_delle_civilt%C3%A0.

The triumph of liberal democracy coincided with the general privatization of the social sphere and the general 'precarization' of labor activity. Its effect was the violent collapse of 'social civilization', a form of civilization in which the interests of the majority are protected by political regulation and, above all, by education that allows for the suspension of the natural law of the jungle.

Along with many other things, capitalist totalitarianism destroyed public schools. The educational processes that in the second half of the twentieth century motivated human life in an ethical and solidarity sense, promoting humanism and egalitarianism, have been replaced by dehumanizing educational processes: pervasive, pounding, inescapable advertising, digitization dominated by large global corporations that innervate themselves in the cognitive activity of linked humans.

And so the most fantastic effect of conformism ever known was produced: ignorance and advertising superstition eliminated every political rule and every cultural form that did not coincide with the imposition of profit.

The complete financialization of the economy, made possible by digital technologies, has achieved the definitive domination of the abstract over the concrete.

Financial capitalism appeared as an automated system with no alternatives, precarious labor proved incapable of solidarity, and the future appeared definitively encapsulated in the automated present.

In this sense Fukuyama was right: history was over, psychic misery was spreading like a raging forest fire, and subjectivity was subjected to mass psycho-pharmacological dictatorship and pervasive digital approval.

Then came the Catastrophe. After the global-scale convulsions of fall 2019 (the global estallido of Hong Kong, Santiago, Quito, Tehran...) along came the virus.[9]

And the virus created the conditions for the psychic collapse that is now disrupting the world stage.

The chaos blocked the circulation of goods and the continuity of work in a large part of the world, but now the threat of war upsets the concrete chain of production-distribution-consumption and the atomic threat disrupts the depressed imaginary, like a bad dream from which one wakes up only to discover that the bad dream is reality.

Revenge

The inter-white war paradoxically causes the world to divide along unseen lines that have little to do with ideology or geopolitics, and have much to do with the history of colonization and racial exploitation.

---

9   *La convulsione*. (2020, June 4). Not. https://not.neroeditions.com/la-convulsione/.

When the proposal to condemn the Russian invasion was presented to the UN, the most populous countries—India, Pakistan, Indonesia, South Africa—abstained along with China. For the first time, a geopolitical scenario is emerging that runs along the colonial fracture line. The white empires of the past clash or join forces, while the non-white world emerges on the horizon.

Russia is the wild card, the madman, the internal element that works as a way to disarticulate the white world.

Another element gone mad could be Pakistan, squeezed between American pressure and now predominant Chinese influence. Prime Minister Imran Khan has used extreme tones to denounce American interference, and Nawaz Sharif has managed to oust him from the country's government. But the battle in Pakistan has only begun and could soon escalate.

Other elements gone mad can be seen around, no need to even name them. Others will go mad.

The inter-white war of Ukraine is the catalyst for a fracture process between the South and the North of which we are only seeing the first movements.

Sometimes I am reminded of Chairman Mao, of whom I have never been a follower, but who said interesting things. I remember that in the 1960s Mao theorized that soon the suburbs would strangle the metropolis.

The theory was particularly advocated by his trusted squire Lin Piao (who was later eliminated while flying in an airplane a few years later, in 1971), but the vision of the Great Helmsman should be understood as a strategic alliance between the workers of the industrialized world and the proletarian or peasant population of the peripheral countries. The slogan of the Communist International, 'Proletarians of the whole world unite!' was reformulated by the Maoists into 'Proletarians and oppressed peoples unite!'

In those years colonialism seemed to recede, the liberation movements repelled the imperialists, and in 1975 the defeat of the Americans in Vietnam seemed the culminating moment of a process of emancipation.

But things did not go exactly as we had hoped: the defeated colonialism resurrected in new forms, as economic domination, as extractivism, as cultural colonization.

The formula 'the countryside will strangle the cities' can be viewed retrospectively as a strategic alternative to the alliance between industrial workers and peoples impoverished by colonialism. If all goes well, Mao said, there will be an alliance between northern workers and southern peasants. If something goes wrong and the northern workers are defeated, then it will be the oppressed peoples who will strangle imperialist capitalism.

I hope you'll forgive the caricatured simplification, but Mao wasn't joking. The Long March had been just that: the countryside had surrounded the cities until it took over in a predominantly peasant country.

The Chinese cherish the memory of the humiliation inflicted in the mid-nineteenth century by the rising Western powers on the Celestial Empire, peripheralizing it for one hundred and fifty years. And so in the 21st century the peoples impoverished by colonialism, subjected for two centuries to exploitation and humiliation, have begun to strangle the white metropolis in many ways: migration, nationalist tribalism, the tendency to break down the role of the dollar as the dominant monetary function at a global level.

The 'good' strategic perspective has failed because the communism of the industrial workers has been defeated by neoliberal global capitalism. Therefore, only the second, more evil one remains: resurgent nationalism, revenge.

For now, revenge is being carried out within the white world, with the conflict between Russia and the 'free world.' But the next chapter is the aggressive re-emergence of the powers subjugated in past centuries.

Can the West survive this double attack that adds to the persistence of Islamist hostility, ready to re-explode in the Middle East, but also in the banlieues of Europe?

Only the internationalism of the working class could have prevented the showdown with the past and present colonialism from resulting in a planetary bloodbath: workers of the industrial West and proletarians of the peoples oppressed by colonialism recognized themselves in the same communist program. But communism has been defeated, and now we must face a free-for-all war in the name of nothing.

Tail

In this general precipice, we must try to imagine the evolution of the European precipice. How will the process of social disintegration agglutinate when the economy is disrupted and society impoverished in a way unthinkable until yesterday? Who will lead the probable European revolts?

At the moment it seems certain that the prevailing forces will be nationalistic and psychotic, and we are reminded of the prediction of Sandor Ferenczi, who in a 1918 paper ruled out that a mass psychosis would be curable.

This is the challenge of today: how do you treat a psychosis that has moved out of its individual limits, and has affected the sphere of the collective mind?

These questions cannot be answered consistently today, yet these questions must be asked urgently, because social subjectivity oscillates between depressive epidemic and aggressive mass psychosis, and only effective treatment for this pathological framework can avoid the terminal Holocaust.

Finding an effective cure is the task of a thought that measures up with the present.

WEAPONIZED OSINT: THE NEW KREMLIN-SPONSORED PARTICIPATORY PROPAGANDA

MARC TUTERS, KARYNA LAZARUK

Image credit: Karyna Lazaruk

'Warfakes' ("Война с фейками") is the name of a popular Russian Telegram channel at the centre of an entire network of related channels that emerged in the opening days of the current Russian invasion of Ukraine. Along with its English language website Waronfakes. com, these channels present themselves as a network that debunks fake news, in a familiar style of fact-checking websites such as PolitiFact. They produce two dozen posts per day on average, where the techniques of open-source intelligence (OSINT) are often used to expose the supposed untruths in the media coverage of the war. These posts are circulated widely on Telegram as well as other social media networks, especially VKontakte. Warfakes represent a new type of disinformation that we refer to as participatory propaganda where users circulate weaponized OSINT, most notably including the Russian state operatives. Here's how authors present themselves:

Welcome to the "War on Fakes" project. We are the owners and administrators of several Russian non-political telegram channels. We don't do politics. But we consider it important to provide unbiased information about what is happening in Ukraine and on the territories of Donbas because we see signs of an information war launched against Russia. Our mission is to make sure that there are only objective publications in the information space. We do not want ordinary people to feel anxious and panicked because of information wars. We are going to look into every fake and give links to the real refutations. Be safe, be at peace, be with us.

Inside the Russian media bubble, debunking sites are just as likely, or even more likely, to 'bunk' news that is true as they are to debunk fake news. While this also happens frequently in broadcast television, Telegram is the most popular fake debunking medium, with the Warfakes channel with over 700k subscribers as its prime example. While the organisation behind Warfakes is unknown, its content is systematically promoted by the Russian state via the Facebook pages of foreign embassies and other Kremlin-sponsored cultural institutions. A close reading of the channels reveals them to consistently promote a number of pro-Kremlin narratives under the guise of questioning sources and exposing apparent discrepancies in reporting.

Warfakes is the largest Russian Telegram channel in a whole genre of other channels that "debunk" war coverage. Compared to other social media, Telegram generally has a softer touch when it comes to censoring content—though this has begun to change recently. Telegram was developed by Pavel Durov after the Kremlin took over his previous social network VKontakte. Telegram's servers are located in the Persian Gulf (after the KGB tried to take it over). Telegram has been referred to as a "dark corner" of the internet (Rogers) due to its light touch approach to moderation. Ultimately, Telegram is a massive platform (with a user base of 400M, which is significantly more than Twitter's 330 users, for example), which makes it hard to generalise as it supports all kinds of communities.

Image credit: Keulenaar & Kisje

On Telegram there are multiple channels with similar names, descriptions and content, which make up a Warfakes network. The channels appeared localised to audiences in specific regions including Ukraine and Belarus and many other smaller Russian-dominated cities and regions (such as Rostov, Belgorod, Cuban, annexed Crimea, Voronizh, Samara, Republic of Kalmykia, Kirov, Khabarovsk region, Zabaykalie, Bashkotorstan, Republic of Sakha). With the main *Warfakes* channel as its core, we identified similar channels as *core clones*. When listing these channels we noticed two prominent groups with the same date of creation: 26.02.2022 and 1.03.2022.

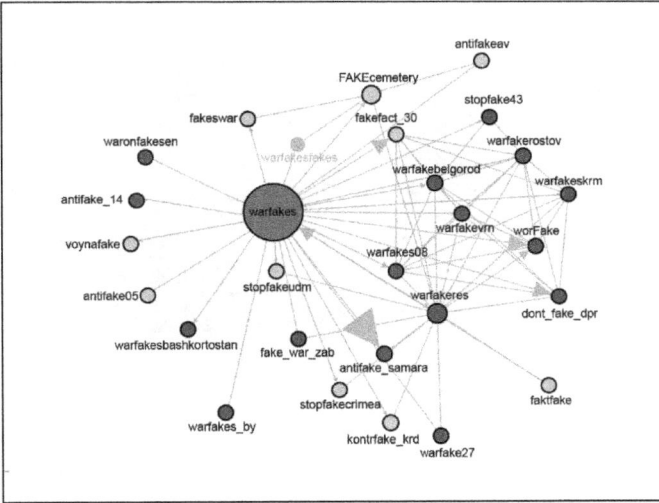

Diagram, schematic

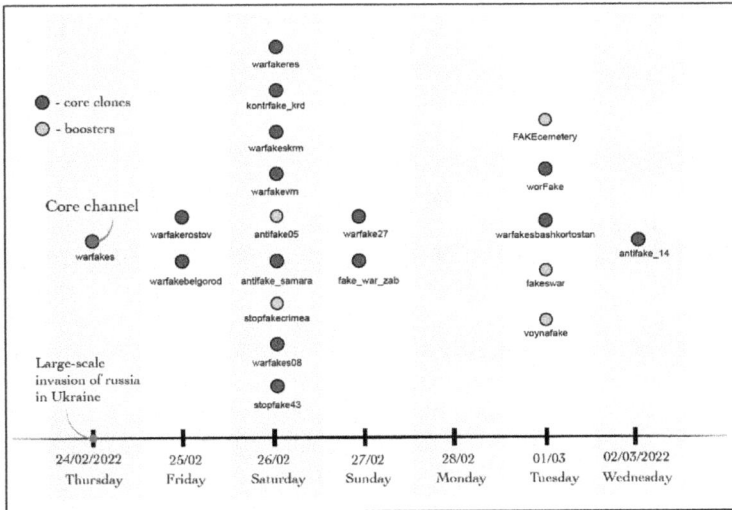

A picture containing timeline

Three levels of fakeness

When conceptualising participatory propaganda, the Warfakes Telegram network has 3 levels of fakeness.

The situation in Bucha. What really happened?

War with fakes. AnalyticsApril • 03, 2022

Despite the fact that information that Russian troops began to leave Bucha appeared on March 31, posts about the large number of abandoned civilian casualties appeared only late in the evening of April 2 and in the morning of April 3.

It is this time lag that causes great suspicion, since earlier the Ukrainian side worked out all such "facts" very quickly and accurately. There is a feeling that this time was used to prepare the largest provocation after the Maruipol Maternity Hospital.

A car driving down a road

The first level is *rhetorical*, where the site uses the rhetoric of fact-checking to identify 'fake' information that is usually not misinformation. This technique is not unique to Warfakes. In fact, this is a popular format on Russian TV as well and was used in a program called 'Antifake' (Starr 2022) as well.[1] On Warfakes, the typical rhetorical structure for 'debunking' is to flag news as *fake* and to then counter it with the (fake) *truth*, accompanied by an *explanation* and a *visual*. Since Telegram is a more participatory medium than TV, Warfakes propaganda has a participatory flavour. As such, the second level of fakeness is *aesthetic*. Much content on Warfakes has a specific "investigative aesthetic" (Weisman and Fuller 2021), where red circles are used to

---

1 *Francis Scarr on Russian TV's Antifake programme.* (2022, April 5). [Tweet]. Twitter. https://twitter.com/francis_scarr/status/1511271292367953920.

identify an image as a supposed deep fake, for example. On Warfakes, the vernacular term for using investigative aesthetics to debunk images is called "creo".[2]

As discussed by Eyal Weisman and Matthew Fuller, investigative aesthetics is a collective practice of using open sources to produce actionable intelligence. They describe investigative aesthetics as "scraps of information [...] compiled into systems, including narrative structures, that allow for their cross-checking and public presentation". Warfakes appropriates the authority of investigative aesthetics to manufacture misinformation. One of the most prominent "investigative aesthetics" operations, Bellingcat (currently based in Amsterdam & Berlin), involves a network of 60+ collaborators who have produced important intelligence in the last few years (the Russian involvement in 2018 Skripal poisoning, for example). Judging from its style and high volume of posts, Warfakes looks like it is being produced by a decentralised network of open-source investigators. However, we simply do not know if this is the case. It could also be produced in a single office, such as Saint Petersburg's infamous Internet Research Agency. Either way, one thing is clear; the content produced here promotes a pro-Kremin version of the war.

The third level of fakeness at work in the case of Warfakes is the *narrative*. Through a process of qualitative data analysis by trained coders, the top 8% of the most engaged with content (141 of a total of 1731 posts) of the Warfakes core channel were selected (from the 24th of February to the 20th of March 2022). A close reading revealed nine narratives:

---

2   *Война с фейками*. (2022, March 8). [Telegram post]. Telegram. https://t.me/warfakes/931.

Denial of war crimes: against civilians and civilian infrastructure: 27, 66% of the analysed content
Blaming and accusing Ukrainians fakes/discrediting: 22,7%
Denial of failures and misery of the russian army: 18%
Blaming and accusing of making up sanctions against Russia: 13,48%
Denying mobilization of russian people: 5,67%
Denying victories of the Ukrainian army: 4,96%
Discrediting President Vladymyr Zelenskij: 3,55%
Blaming and accusing Ukrainians of Nazism: 2,84%
Biolaboratories in Ukraine: 0,71%

We found that the most popular "debunked" narratives were about the Russian army's worst atrocity to that date*: 1.) the missile attacks on a maternity house and children's hospital in Mariupol 2.) the attack on a drama theatre in Mariupol and 3.) the killing of journalist Brent Renaud.

Three months after the first analysis we performed the same close reading of a wider scope of 10% of the most engaged content and found nine new narratives:

Deterioration of life in the world because of Ukraine
Discrediting the Armed Forces of Ukraine
NATO assistance is ineffective and leads to a bigger war
Russians are interested in the topic of "special operations" and / or support it
Denial of support for Ukraine by other countries or initiatives
Life under occupation is good and peaceful
European countries cannot be trusted
Russia is friendly to refugees and residents of the occupied territories
Recognition of "LDNR" as a legal territory

During the first three months of the Russian full-scale invasion denying war crimes and blaming Ukrainians for creating fakes were the narratives that were used most frequently. The debunking of the worst atrocities, such as the Bucha massacre, were also the most popular.

Warfakes as State-Sponsored Propaganda

In the course of analysing who reposted Warfakes content, we found that from the 24th of February until the 28th of March in 2022, the director of the Information and Press Department of the MFA RF, Maria Zakharova's, reposted Warfakes content from her own verified Telegram channel. The first post promoted waronfakes.com and the second was a repost of their 'debunking' of the Russian army's bombing of the Mariupol maternity ward. Later we observed that the telegram channel of the Ministry of Defence of Russia made 264 mentions of the Warfakes (as of 30.07.2022). Using the Meta research tool Crowdtangle, we investigated all mentions of the Warfakes TG channel on Facebook. We found that the main promoters of Warfakes content were Russian embassies and Russian houses of culture, both of which are under the jurisdiction of the Russian Ministry of Foreign Affairs. Each of these Facebook pages had 9800 subscribers (from 49471 to 594) on average, and each post had an engagement rate from 1482 to 5.

Spreading Warfakes channel on Facebook by Russian houses as of the 22nd of March 2022:

1. Sofia	9. Zagreb	17. Tunisia
2. Belgrade	10. Romania	18. Alexandria
3. Chisinau	11. Skopje	19. Chennai
4. Ankara	12. Bishkek	20. Podgorica
5. Beirut	13. Amman	21. Vein
6. Prague	14. New Delhi	22. Brest
7. Cairo	15. Yerevan	23. Dar es Salaam
8. Athens	16. Bratislava	

Spreading Warfakes channel on Facebook by Russian embassies as of the 22nd of March 2022:

1. Bulgaria	5. Slovenia	9. Montenegro
2. Sweden	6. Laos	10. Kazakhst
3. Macedonia	7. Denmark	
4. România	8. Israel	

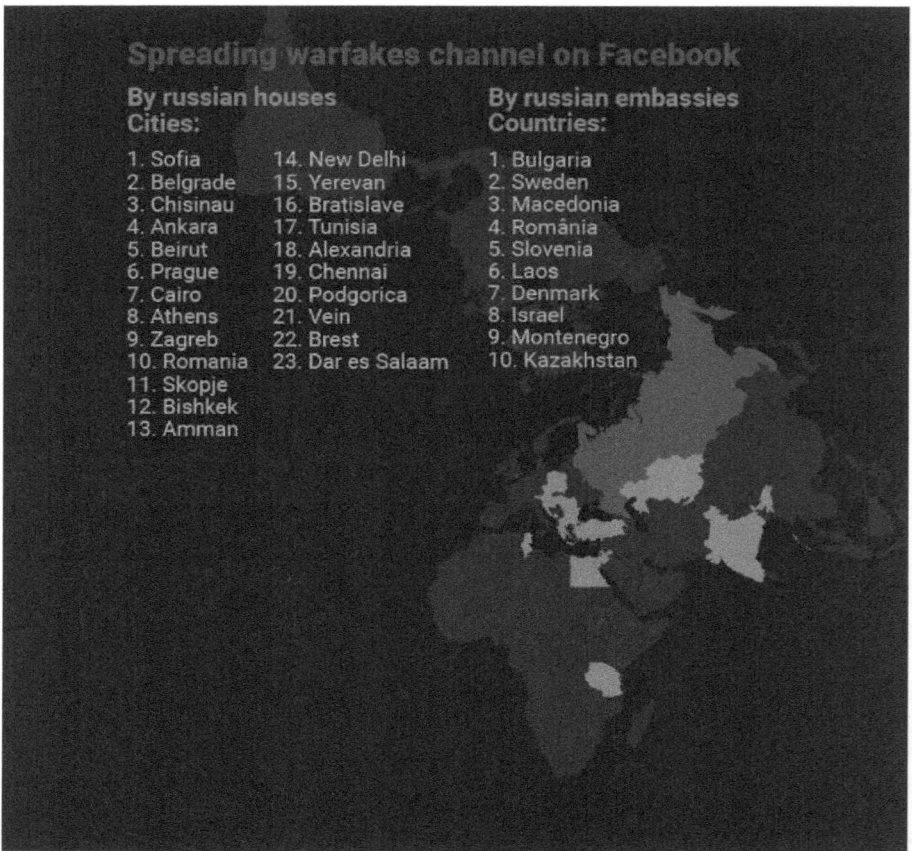

Image credit: Karyna Lazaruk

Screenshot from tgstats.ru with the most frequent interaction (incoming and outgoing) between channels.

Warfakes as participatory propaganda

Warfakes is a new form of propaganda that is participatory, as opposed to 'traditional' propaganda, which is usually top-down. By definition, participatory propaganda is co-produced by users to some extent. While we do not know who makes the content on Telegram, a crucial affordance of the medium is sharing. As such, part of what makes this propaganda so successful is how it spreads, including users sharing the content who may not agree with it.

Warfakes should be considered in the broader context of the Russian disinformation strategy. This can be traced back to Putin's reaction to the UN-backed war in Libya and Maidan protests. In order to avoid his own uprising, state-sponsored influence operations have developed these new forms of participatory propaganda.

Their strategy is to create epistemological confusion that causes people to question the idea of objective truth. This benefits reactionary nationalistic narratives. Since Maidan, Russia's military has developed a new "Gerasimov doctrine" in which future wars would take place mostly in the information space. Therefore, it seems reasonable to speculate that Warfakes may in fact be a Russian military operation.

Telegram's ownership tried to resist state control in the past, but the platform is being used by the Kremlin. We believe they should take responsibility and remove the channels.

This article was based on the findings of the project executed during the Digital Methods Winter School in 2022 in Amsterdam. Participants: Karyna Lazaruk and Marc Tuters (project leaders), Borka Balogh, Marta Ceccarelli, Emillie de Keulenaar, Kiara Khorram, Devin Mitter, Son Nguyen, Stijn Peeters, Emilie Schwantzer, Cemal Tahir, Alexander Teggin, Yana Mashkova, and Anton Mishchuk.

FIGHTING DISINFORMATION: WE'RE SOLVING THE WRONG PROBLEMS

MICHAŁ "RYSIEK" WOŹNIAK

Tackling disinformation and misinformation is a problem that is important, timely, hard and... in no way new. Throughout history, different forms of propaganda, manipulation, and biased reporting have been present and deployed — consciously or not; maliciously or not — to steer political discourse and to goad public outrage. The issue has admittedly become more urgent lately and we do need to do something about it. I believe, however, that so far we've been focusing on the wrong parts of it.

Consider the term 'fake news' itself. It feels like a new invention even though its literal use was first recorded in 1890.[1] On the surface it means "news that is untrue", but of course it has been twisted and abused to claim that certain factual reporting is false or manufactured—to a point where its very use might suggest that a person using it is not being entirely forthright.[2]

That's the crux of it; in a way, 'fake' is in the eye of the beholder.

Matter of trust

While it is possible to *define* misinformation and disinformation, any such definition necessarily *relies on things that are not easy (or possible) to quickly verify*: a news item's relation to truth, and its authors' or distributors intent.[3]

This is especially valid within any domain that deals with complex knowledge that is highly nuanced, especially when stakes are high and emotions heat up. Public debate around COVID-19 is a chilling example. Regardless of how much 'own research' anyone has done, for those without advanced medical and scientific background it eventually boiled down to the question of 'who do you trust'. Some trusted medical professionals, some didn't (and still don't).

As the world continues to assess the harrowing consequences of the pandemic, it is clear that the misinformation around and disinformation campaigns about it had a real cost, expressed in needless human suffering and lives lost.

---

1   'Editors of Merriam-Webster. (2022, May 23). *How Is "Fake News" Defined, and When Will It Be Added to the Dictionary?* The Merriam-Webster.Com Dictionary. https://www.merriam-webster.com/words-at-play/the-real-story-of-fake-news.
2   Nordlinger, J. (2019, March 18). *'Fake News,' They Say*. National Review. https://www.nationalreview.com/corner/fake-news-they-say/.
3   For the definitions of misinformation and disinformation, as provided by Merriam-Webster dictionary, see: 'Misinformation Definition', https://www.merriam-webster.com/dictionary/misinformation, and 'Disinformation Definition', https://www.merriam-webster.com/dictionary/disinformation.

It is tempting, therefore, to call for censorship or other sanctions against misinformation and disinformation peddlers. And indeed, in many places legislation is already in place that punishes them with fines or jail time. These places include Turkey and Russia, and it will surprise no-one that media organizations are sounding alarm about them.[4]

The Russian case is especially relevant here. On one hand the Russian state insists on calling their war of aggression against Ukraine a 'special military operation' and blatantly lies about losses sustained by the Russian armed forces, and about war crimes committed by them.[5] On the other hand, the Kremlin appoints itself the arbiter of truth and demands that any news organizations in Russia propagate these lies on its behalf—using "anti-fake news" laws as leverage.

Disinformation peddlers are not just trying to push specific narratives. The broader aim is to discredit the very idea that there can at all exist *any* reliable, trustworthy information source.[6] After all, if nothing is trustworthy, the disinformation peddlers themselves are as trustworthy as it gets. The target is trust itself.

And so we apparently find ourselves in an impossible position:

On one hand, the global pandemic, a war in Eastern Europe, and the climate crisis are all complex, emotionally charged high-stakes issues that can easily be exploited by peddlers of misinformation and disinformation, which thus become existential threats that urgently need to be dealt with.

On the other hand, in many ways, the cure might be worse than the disease. "Anti-fake news" laws can, just like libel laws, enable malicious actors to stifle truthful but inconvenient reporting, to the detriment of the public debate, and the debating public.[7] Employing censorship to fight disinformation and misinformation is fraught with peril.

I believe that we are looking for solutions to the wrong aspects of the problem. Instead of trying to legislate misinformation and disinformation away, we should instead be looking closely at

---

4   'Deutsche Welle (www.dw.com). (2022, May 31). *Turkey seeks to tighten media control with "fake news" bill*. DW.COM. https://www.dw.com/en/turkey-seeks-to-tighten-media-control-with-fake-news-bill/a-61990381.
5   Bort, C. (2022, January 6). Why The Kremlin Lies: Understanding Its Loose Relationship With the Truth. Carnegie Endowment for International Peace. https://carnegieendowment.org/2022/01/06/why-kremlin-lies-understanding-its-loose-relationship-with-truth-pub-86132.
    Faulconbridge, G. (2022, April 5). Kremlin says Bucha is "monstrous forgery" aimed at smearing Russia. Reuters. https://www.reuters.com/world/europe/putin-ally-says-bucha-killings-are-fake-propaganda-2022-04-05/.
6   Paul, C., & Matthews, M. (2016). The Russian "Firehose of Falsehood" Propaganda Model: Why It Might Work and Options to Counter It. *The Russian "Firehose of Falsehood" Propaganda Model*. https://doi.org/10.7249/pe198.
7   Siddique, H. (2022, June 14). Arron Banks loses libel action against reporter Carole Cadwalladr. *The Guardian*. https://www.theguardian.com/uk-news/2022/jun/13/arron-banks-loses-libel-action-against-reporter-carole-cadwalladr-guardian-defamation-brexit-russia.

how it is possible that it spreads so fast (and who benefits from this). We should be finding ways to fix the media funding crisis; also we should be making sure that future generations receive the mental tools that would allow them to cut through biases, hoaxes, rhetorical tricks, and logical fallacies weaponized to wage information wars.

Compounding the problem

The reason why misinformation and disinformation spreads so fast is because our most commonly used communication tools have been built in a way that promotes that kind of content over fact-checked, long-form, nuanced reporting.

According to the Washington Post, "Facebook programmed the algorithm that decides what people see in their news feeds to use the reaction emoji as signals to push more emotional and provocative content—including content likely to make them angry."[8]

When this is combined with the fact that "[Facebook's] data scientists confirmed in 2019 that posts that sparked [the] angry reaction emoji were disproportionately likely to include misinformation, toxicity and low-quality news", you get a tool fine-tuned to spread misinformation and disinformation. What's worse, the more people get angry at a particular post, the more it spreads. The more angry commenters point out how false it is, the more the algorithm promotes it to others.

One could call this the "outrage dividend", and disinformation benefits especially handsomely from it.[9] It is related to "yellow journalism", the type of journalism where newspapers present little or no legitimate, well-researched news while instead using eye-catching headlines for increased sales, of course.[10] The difference is that tabloids of the early 20th century didn't get the additional boost from a global communication system effectively *designed* to promote this kind of content.

I am not saying Facebook *intentionally designed* its platform to become the best tool a malicious disinformation actor could dream of. This might have been (and probably was) an innocent mistake, an unintended consequence of the way the post-promoting algorithm was supposed to work.

But in large systems even tiny mistakes compound to become huge problems, especially over time. And Facebook happens to be a gigantic system that has been with us for almost two decades. In the immortal words of fictional Senator Soaper: "To err is human, but to really foul things up you need a computer."[11]

8   Merrill, J. B., & Oremus, W. (2021, October 26). 'Five points for anger, one for a 'like': How Facebook's formula fostered rage and misinformation', *Washington Post*. https://www.washingtonpost.com/technology/2021/10/26/facebook-angry-emoji-algorithm/.

9   Woźniak, M. (2022, June 29). *The Outrage Dividend*. Songs on the Security of Networks. https://rys.io/en/159.html.

10   Wikipedia contributors. (2022, June 27). *Yellow journalism*. Wikipedia. https://en.wikipedia.org/wiki/Yellow_journalism.

11   Quoteresearch, A. (2010, December 7). *To Err is Human; To Really Foul Things Up Requires a Computer – Quote Investigator*. Quote Investigator. https://quoteinvestigator.com/2010/12/07/foul-computer/.

Of course the solution is not as simple as just telling Facebook and other social media platforms not to do this. What we need (among other things) is algorithmic transparency, so that we can reason about *how* and *why* exactly a particular piece of content gets promoted.[12]

More importantly, we also need to decentralize our online areas of public debate.[13] The current situation in which we consume (and publish) most of our news through two or three global companies, who effectively have full control over our feeds and over our ability to reach our audiences, is untenable. Monopolized, centralized social media is a monoculture where mind viruses can spread unchecked.[14]

It's worth noting that these monopolistic monocultures (in both the policy and software sense) are a very enticing target for anyone who would be inclined to maliciously exploit the algorithm's weaknesses. The post-promoting algorithm is, after all, just software, and all software has bugs. If you find a way to game the system, you get to reach incredibly numerous audiences. It should then come as no surprise that most vaccine hoaxes on social media can be traced back to only 12 people.[15]

Centralization obviously also relates to the ability of billionaires to just buy a social network wholesale, or the inability (or unwillingness) of mainstream social media platforms to deal with abuse and extremism.[16] They all stem from the fact that a handful of for-profit companies control daily communication of several billion people. This is too few companies to wield that kind of power, especially when they demonstrably wield it so badly.[17]

Alternatives do already exist. Fediverse,[18] a decentralized social network, does not have a single company controlling it (and no shady algorithm deciding who gets to see which posts), and does not have to come up with a single set of rules for everyone on it (an impossible task, as former Twitter CEO, Jack Dorsey, admits).[19] Its decentralized nature (there are thousands of servers run by different people and groups, with different rules) means that it's easier to deal

12   Wikipedia contributors. (2021, December 11). *Algorithmic transparency*. Wikipedia. https://en.wikipedia.
     org/wiki/Algorithmic_transparency.
13   Woźniak, M. (2021, February 22). Centralisation is a danger to democracy. VSQUARE.ORG. https://
     vsquare.org/centralisation-is-a-danger-to-democracy/.
14   Rysiekúr Memesson (@rysiek@mastodon.technology). (2021, July 10). [Mastodon post]. Mastodon for
     Tech Folks. https://mastodon.technology/@rysiek/106556809919924178.
15   *NPR Cookie Consent and Choices*. (2021, May 13). Npr.Org. https://choice.npr.org/index.
     html?origin=https://www.npr.org/2021/05/13/996570855/disinformation-dozen-test-facebooks-
     twitters-ability-to-curb-vaccine-hoaxes?t=1656680064488&t=1657462345986.
16   'Taylor, J. (2022, April 26). Elon Musk's Twitter takeover: what will change, is free speech at risk and
     should you delete the app? *The Guardian*. https://www.theguardian.com/technology/2022/apr/26/elon-
     musk-twitter-takeover-bought-buys-what-will-change-is-free-speech-at-risk.
     Kamps, H. J. (2019, October 13). Solving Twitter's abuse problem - Haje Jan Kamps. Medium. https://
     haje.medium.com/solving-twitter-s-abuse-problem-3f1f8ac1a0d2.
17   Pierce, D., & Kramer, A. (2021, October 28). Here are all the Facebook Papers stories. Protocol. https://
     www.protocol.com/facebook-papers.
18   'fediverse.info. (2022). Fediverse. https://fediverse.info.
19   *jack on centrilization and misinformation*. (2019, December 11). [Tweet]. Twitter. https://twitter.com/
     jack/status/1204766082206011393.

with abuse.[20] And since it's not controlled by a single for-profit company there is no incentive to keep bad actors in so as not to risk an outflow of users (and thus a drop in stock prices).[21]

So, we can start by at least setting up a presence in the Fediverse right now (following thousands of users who migrated there after Elon Musk's Twitter bid).[22] And we can push for centralized social media walled gardens to be forced to open their protocols, so that their owners no longer can keep us hostage.[23] Just like the ability to move a number between mobile providers makes it easier for us to switch while keeping in touch with our contacts, the ability to communicate *across* different social networks would make it easier to transition out of the walled gardens without losing our *audience*.

Media funding

As far as funding is concerned, entities spreading disinformation have at least three advantages over reliable media and fact-checking organizations.

First, they can be bank-rolled by actors who do not care if they turn a profit.[24] Secondly, they don't have to spend any money on actual reporting, research, fact-checking, and everything else that is both *required* and *costly* in an honest news outlet. Third, as opposed to a lot of nuanced long-form journalism, disinformation benefits greatly from the aforementioned "outrage dividend"—it is *easier* for disinformation to get the clicks, and create ad revenues.

Meanwhile, honest media organizations are squeezed from every possible side. Not the least by the very platforms that gate-keep their reach, or provide (and pay for) ads on their websites.

Many organizations, including small public grant-funded outlets, find themselves in a position where they feel they *have to* pay Facebook for 'reach'; to promote their posts on its platform. They don't benefit from the outrage dividend, after all.

In other words, money that would otherwise go into paying journalists working for a small, often embattled media organization, gets funneled to one of the biggest tech companies in

20 Caelin, D. (2020, October 19). *Decentralized Social Networks vs. The Trolls.* SocialHub. https://socialhub. activitypub.rocks/t/decentralized-social-networks-vs-the-trolls/941.
21 Panetta, G. (2019, April 26). *Twitter reportedly won't use an algorithm to crack down on white supremacists because some GOP politicians could end up getting barred too.* Business Insider. https:// www.businessinsider.com/twitter-algorithm-crackdown-white-supremacy-gop-politicians-report-2019-4?r=US&IR=T.
22 Pardes, A. (2022, April 28). *What Elon Musk Can Learn From Mastodon—and What He Can't.* Wired. https://www.wired.com/story/elon-musk-twitter-masatodon/.
23 Masonic, M. (2019, August 21). *Protocols, Not Platforms: A Technological Approach to Free Speech.* Knight First Amendment Institute. https://knightcolumbia.org/content/protocols-not-platforms-a-technological-approach-to-free-speech.
24 Cvetkovska, S., Belford, A., Silverman, C., & Lester Feder, J. (2018, July 18). *The Secret Players Behind Macedonia's Fake News Sites.* OCCRP. https://www.occrp.org/en/spooksandspin/the-secret-players-behind-macedonias-fake-news-sites.

the world, which consciously built their system as a "roach motel"[25]—easy to get in, very hard to get out once you start using it—and now exploits that to extract payments for "reach". An economist might call it "monopolistic rent-seeking".[26]

Meanwhile, the biggest ad networks operator, Google, uses their similar near-monopoly position to extract an ever larger share of ad revenues, leaving less and less on the table for media organizations that rely on them for their ads.[27]

All this means that as time goes by it gets progressively harder to publish quality fact-checked news. This is again tied to centralization, giving a few Big Tech companies the ability to control global information flow, and extract rents from that.

A move to non-targeted, contextual ads might be worth a shot—some studies show that targeted advertising offers quite limited gains compared to other forms of advertising.[28] At the same time, cutting out the rent-seeking middle man leaves a larger slice of the pie on the table for publishers.[29] More public funding (perhaps funded by a tax levied on the mega-platforms) is also an idea worth considering.[30]

Media education

Finally, we need to make sure our audiences can understand what they're reading, along with the fact that somebody might have vested interests in writing a post or an article in a particular way.[31] We cannot have that without robust media literacy education in schools.

Logic and rhetoric have long been banished from most public schools as, apparently, they are not useful for finding a job. Logical fallacies are barely (if at all) covered. At the same time both misinformation and disinformation rely heavily on logical fallacies. I will not be at all original when I say that school curricula need to emphasize critical thinking, but it still needs to be said.

---

25   Doctorow, C. (2021, April 5). *Cory Doctorow on Facebook* [Tweet]. Twitter. https://twitter.com/doctorow/status/1379070922594820097.
26   (2020, November 3). *Exploring economic rents and algorithmic monopolies in the digital*. UCL Institute for Innovation and Public Purpose. https://www.ucl.ac.uk/bartlett/public-purpose/research-projects/2020/nov/exploring-economic-rents-and-algorithmic-monopolies-digital-economy.
27   McCabe, D., & Wakabayashi, D. (2020, December 17). '10 States Accuse Google of Abusing Monopoly in Online Ads', *The New York Times*. https://www.nytimes.com/2020/12/16/technology/google-monopoly-antitrust.html.
28   Hagey, K. (2019, May 29). *Behavioral Ad Targeting Not Paying Off for Publishers, Study Suggests*. WSJ. https://www.wsj.com/articles/behavioral-ad-targeting-not-paying-off-for-publishers-study-suggests-11559167195.
29   Lomas, N. (2020, July 24). *TechCrunch is part of the Yahoo family of brands*. Techcrunch.Com. https://techcrunch.com/2020/07/24/data-from-dutch-public-broadcaster-shows-the-value-of-ditching-creepy-ads/?guccounter=1.
30   Martin, E. (2019, May 10). *Should We Tax Big Tech Companies to Pay for Local Journalism?* Protego Press. https://www.protegopress.com/should-we-tax-big-tech-companies-to-pay-for-local-journalism/.
31   Watson, L. (2018) *'Systematic Epistemic Rights Violations in the Media: A Brexit Case Study'*, Social Epistemology 32 2, pp. 88-102.

We also need to update the way we teach, to fit the current world. Education is still largely built around the idea that information is scarce and the main difficulty is acquiring it (hence its focus on memorizing facts and figures). Meanwhile, for at least a decade if not more, information is plentiful, and the difficulty lies in filtering it and figuring out which information sources to trust.

Solving the right problem, together

"Every complex problem has a solution which is simple, direct, plausible—and wrong", observed H. L. Mencken. This describes the push for seemingly simple solutions to the misinformation and disinformation crisis, like legislation making disinformation (however defined) "illegal", quite well.

News and fact-checking communities have limited resources. We cannot afford to spend them on ineffective solutions—and much less on fighting about proposals that are both highly controversial and recognized broadly as dangerous.

To really deal with this crisis we need to recognize centralization—of social media, of ad networks, of media ownership, of power over our daily communication, and in many other areas related to news publishing—and poor media literacy among the public as crucial underlying causes that need to be tackled.

Once we do, we have options. Those mentioned in this text are just rough ideas; there are bound to be many more. But we need to start by focusing on the right parts of the problem.

NOT ALL CRITICISM IS RUSSOPHOBIC: ON DECOLONIAL APPROACH TO RUSSIAN CULTURE.

LIA DOSTLIEVA AND ANDRII DOSTLIEV

The text was originally published in BLOK *in March 2022. Here, the text is republished with the author's consent.*

It was already the second week of the full-scale Russian war against Ukraine when one of our Western European friends, a well-known artist and curator, reached out: "Hey Lia, how are you? I'm going to organize an antiwar exhibition where Ukrainian and Russian artists will be presented together, protesting against Putin and his war. I need your help on this one".

He was surprised and disappointed by my immediate negative response. After a long conversation, it became clear that it was impossible to explain to him what was wrong with the "Ukrainians and Russians standing together against Putin and his war" approach. I felt helpless seeing how all my arguments failed to change his mind, and that he was clearly repelled by my stance. "I'm trying to understand you, but I completely reject the idea of nationalism", he wrote. Later that day when I met with my Polish colleagues I was still shaken. I told them about this dialogue and they reacted the way I knew they would—to them it was obvious what is wrong with this type of joint events in times of war.

On one hand, the full-scale Russian military invasion of Ukraine, has attracted a unique amount of attention to Ukraine from all over the world, but on the other hand, it has already been demonstrated that this attention does not necessarily come with the ability to hear and to understand. The war has unearthed the problem that should have been addressed a long time ago: in the whirlwind of statements on the war in Ukraine, not all voices are heard equally. Even today, the hierarchy of the rights to exercise agency still reflects the colonial narratives, and it results in the unpreparedness to accept Ukrainian voices as equal. Let us go back for a moment to the CBS reporter calling Ukraine a "relatively civilized, relatively European" place, where one wouldn't expect to see a war happening, in comparison to Iraq or Afghanistan, where the conflicts have been going on for decades.[1] Aside from the openly racist nature of this commentary, it suggests that military invasion can only happen to the "uncivilized places", thus paradoxically stripping agency from the society that is invaded.

But if Western colonialism and entitlement have been thoroughly analyzed and described over the last forty years, and the necessity of applying decolonial approaches when discussing relationships with the so-called West is no longer perceived as controversial, the understanding of Russian culture as imperialistic and colonial in its nature still remains a rather marginal line of thought.

---

1   Lambert, H. (2022, February 27). *CBS Reporter Criticized for "Civilized" Ukraine Comments*. TheWrap. https://www.thewrap.com/cbs-charlie-dagata-backlash-ukraine-civilized/.

Ewa Thompson in *Imperial knowledge. Russian Literature and Colonialism* notes that in Russia, the process of deconstruction of the imperial myth didn't happen because it was believed that Russian imperialism was a question of the pre-communist past.[2] The postcolonial discourse focused on former Western colonies and the support they were receiving from the Soviet Union, not on the similarity of colonial practices of tsarist and soviet regimes. After the dissolution of the Soviet Union, the joy of seeing tyranny fall forced many smaller issues out of public discussion and the heritage of Russian colonialism in Russian literature and culture evaded criticism altogether. Russian literature had created a strong non-colonial image in the perceptions of western readers. Other voices were seldom heard—and if they did surface, they were easily dismissed.

Centuries of destruction of Ukrainian culture remain totally out of focus. The exact name used by the colonial power in each of those episodes of repressions is of little importance, be it the Russian Empire, the Soviet Union, or the Russian Federation. The important thing is that the attitude of this entity towards the Ukrainian national project was the same: its very existence was not allowed. And to ensure this, all means were used; from the prohibition of the use of the Ukrainian language to the physical destruction of its speakers.

Let us recall the Valuev Circular of 1863, which stated that "a separate Little Russian language [as they used to call Ukrainian then – L.D. & A.D.] never existed, does not exist, and shall not exist, and their tongue used by commoners is nothing but Russian corrupted by the influence of Poland", and the Ems Ukaz which completely prohibited the use of the Ukrainian language in open print in 1876.

Let us also recall the man-made famine of 1932–1933, orchestrated by the Soviet regime, which caused the death of almost 4 million people in the territory of Soviet Ukraine.

Let us recall Sandarmokh, a place in Karelia, where in 1937 NKVD executed 1,111 people, among them were the most prominent representatives of the Ukrainian intellectual elite: Les Kurbas, an innovative theater director and creator of the Berezil Theater; writer Mykola Kulish, philosopher and novelist Valerian Pidmohylny, poets, writers, and translators Mykola Zerov, Pavlo Fylypovych, Valerian Polishchuk, Hryhorii Epik, Myroslav Irchan, Marko Vorony, Mikhailo Kozoris, Oleksa Slisarenko, Mykhailo Yalovy, geographer Stepan Rudnytskyi, historian Matvii Yavorskyi, and many others.

---

2   Thompson, E. M. (2000). *Imperial Knowledge: Russian Literature and Colonialism (Contributions to the Study of World Literature)* (First Edition). Greenwood Press.

Collage by Andriy Gryschuk using the photo by Mark McKinnon of a kindergarten in Stanytsia Luhanska shelled on February 17.

Neither Putin's speech preceding the invasion (where he stated that the very idea of Ukrainian statehood was a fiction), nor the invasion itself are something new or unseen—they are merely the next steps in a long history of the Russian colonial perception of Ukraine and Ukrainian culture as a threat that has to be destroyed.

Regardless of this, there are still numerous voices, especially among the 'westerners', calling for the separation of Russian culture from what they call 'Putin's aggression'. One of the most illustrious examples of such shortsightedness is the open letter by PEN-Deutschland, which explicitly states that "the enemy is Putin, not Pushkin or Tolstoy", and in regard to the calls for boycotting Russian culture notes that "if we allow ourselves to be carried away by such reflexes, by generalizations and hostility against Russians, madness has triumphed, reason and humanity have lost."[3] Thus, not only does this statement infantilize the whole of Russian society and redirect the guilt of warmongering onto a single person, but also, on a larger scale, it seems to completely ignore the fact that precisely Pushkin and precisely Tolstoy—among many others—were vocal promoters of the Russian imperial myth and colonial wars.

The historical lack of understanding of Russian culture as imperial and colonial by nature, and of

---

3   *The enemy is Putin, not Pushkin.* (2022, March 6). PEN-Zentrum Deutschland. https://www.pen-deutschland.de/de/2022/03/06/the-enemy-is-putin-not-pushkin/.

its bearers as people who belong to a privileged group, along with the firmly engraved perception of Russian culture being more important in comparison with the cultures of neighbouring countries has resulted in the current Western belief that the suffering of Ukrainians, killed by Russian artillery and bombing, are largely equal to the inconveniences of Russian civilians. Through this lens, both Ukrainians and Russians are equally considered to be the victims of Putin's criminal regime. Thus, we see a rise in Western emergency residencies and scholarships for artists and scholars from Ukraine AND Russia. We also see plenty of panel discussions on the ongoing war where Western organizers invite participants both from Ukraine and Russia.

Moreover, the responses to sanctions imposed on Russia and the calls for boycotting its culture more and more frequently come with accusations of discrimination, 'russophobia', and hatred. Thus, a reaction directly caused by military aggression becomes reframed as unprovoked hatred of an ethnic group.

In a new music video by the Russian band Leningrad, today's position of Russians is compared to the position of Jews in Berlin in 1940. To illustrate this comparison, people in the video wear traditional Russian kosovorotkas with makeshift Stars of David attached to them. Such an interpretation is a blatant insult to the memory of the victims of the Shoah. Moreover, the rhetoric of the band discursively coincides with the manipulative methods of Russian propaganda.

Ленинград — Входа нет!

Leningrad—No Entry!![4]

Another illustration of Russian culture being inseparable from Russian politics are the photos staged by the Ballet Theater in Russian-occupied Donetsk. For this photoshoot, that was used

---

4   *Ленинград — Входа нет!* (2022, March 10). [Video]. YouTube. *https://www.youtube.com/watch?v=FeIjDxbAZeM*.

by Russian media to demonstrate support for the war in Ukraine, the ballerinas formed huge letters *Z* and *V* on stage. These letters, marked on Russian military vehicles taking part in the invasion, are being widely used by Russia as symbols of this war. Ballet has always been one of the cornerstones of Russian cultural identity and one of its most prominent cultural exports. But it is also historically entangled in the Russian imperialistic narrative and is clearly still being used as a medium to broadcast its messages.

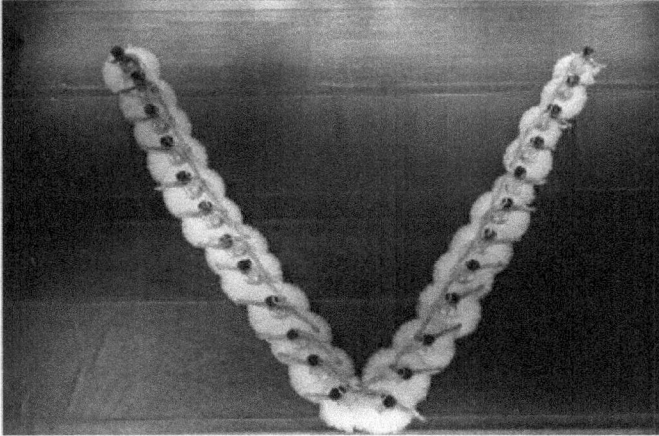

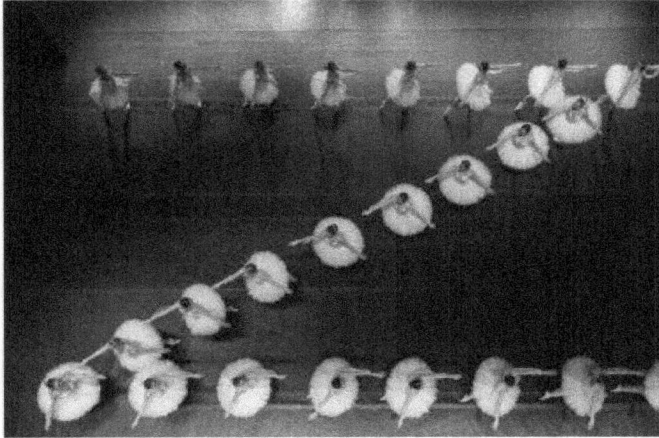

Ballerinas of the Donetsk Theater lined up in the letters Z and V in support of the Russian Federation's special operation[5].

Aside from the examples of Russian culture being a tool of state propaganda, with all of

---

5   Иванов, Н. (2022, March 14). *Балерины Донецкого театра выстроились в буквы Z и V в поддержку спецоперации РФ*. Ямал-Медиа. https://yamal-media.ru/news/baleriny-donetskogo-teatra-pokazali-tanets-v-podderzhku-rossijskoj-spetsoperatsii.

its cannibalistic messages, it's also worth noting that this imperialistic way of thinking can sometimes be employed by those Russian cultural workers who do not support Putin and position themselves as oppositionists. This is usually revealed in online discussions or under Facebook posts by Ukrainian artists.

One example was triggered by artist Alevtyna Kakhidze's Facebook post about the inappropriateness of the participation of Russian artists in a public talk called "Teach-in on Ukraine for artists, activists, and art workers". Alevtyna was encouraging participants from Russia to personally engage in the decolonisation processes and step away from participation in such events in favor of participants from Ukraine. One of those Russian participants, Dmitriy Vilenskiy, had published an open letter about his resignation from the event.[6] But as the reason for his decision he stated that "after spreading information about the event on social media [Russian participants – L.D & A.D.] received a lot of angry messages". Instead of recognising his belonging to a culture that for centuries has been an oppressor, he claimed that "we cannot participate in discussions where [. . .] everything Russian is considered as a culture of oppression and colonization". He also proceeds to patronize Ukrainians about their attitude toward their shared history. So even those who claim to be against the colonial consciousness can still remain its champion.

What can Russian voices bring into public discussions, who is their target audience and who will actually hear it? What can these voices tell Ukrainians that has not already been told by the photographs or personal experiences of destroyed houses, maternity wards, kindergartens in Mariupol, Kharkiv, Chernihiv, Volnovakha, and so on? Can they be something more than an attempt to dissociate from the shared responsibility for this war?

If their messages are directed to their compatriots in Russia, then why do they need a platform in the "civilized" world, where surely few—if any—Russians would hear them? Instead, why not concentrate efforts on spreading anti-war/anti-regime messages inside Russia? Or, maybe, the real target audience of these statements are Western cultural institutions and universities, grantors, curators, collectors,—all of these people who have been providing for the happy lives and career developments of Russian artists and scholars?

If you are a cultural worker from Russia who feels ashamed or guilty for this war and you don't know what to do, start by decolonising your own culture from within or give your place on international platforms to Ukrainian voices. It would surely be uncomfortable and uncanny, but you will not be alone in this. Some of your colleagues are already there.

---

6   Vilensky, D. (2022, March 12). *Open Letter on the Withdrawal from the Teach-In on Ukraine | by Dmitry Vilensky –*. Chtodelat.Org. https://chtodelat.org/b5-announcements/a-6/open-letter-on-the-withdrawal-from-the-teach-in-on-ukraine-by-dmitry-vilensky/.

ENDANGERED PROFESSION

Being a Journalist in Occupied Crimea

ELMAZ ASAN

This is the transcript of the speech Elmaz Asan gave during the Tactical Media Room Meetup at Spui25 on the 30th of June, 2022.

Good evening, dear participants and journalists of such an important event. I am honored to be among you.

Until 2014, as a journalist, I could not even have imagined for what kind of truth, for information that is based on real events and, eventually for your opinion, for your position, you can now suffer. You can receive a warning notice from the punitive authorities because you want to honor the memory of your ancestors in your native land.

However, lies and disinformation are actively encouraged there by the occupying regime.

After the aggression of the Russian invasion of Crimea in 2014, the editorial offices of independent media were searched, and the Crimean Tatar TV channel *ATP* was not spared.

The profession of an independent and objective journalist became a dangerous career choice under the occupation. Free media, which did not submit to the invaders, had to leave the peninsula due to the systematic pressure, threats, and searches both in the editorial offices and in the homes of journalists and news correspondents.

After 2014, my colleagues, journalists from among the Crimean Tatars, suffered to a greater extent. Our people opposed the occupation and did not accept the occupying power that was established in 2014.

I want to give you a few examples of what happened to my fellow journalists after 2014 and of what is still happening on the peninsula. In the first days of the occupation of Crimea, my colleague Ibraim Umerov, when he was fulfilling his professional duty by filming the seizure of the Bogdan-Avto car dealership, was attacked by armed people. All this happened during a live broadcast, but this did not stop the Russian invaders. Ibraim was beaten, his phone was taken away so that he could not contact anyone, and the operator's equipment was taken away.

I must also tell you about a journalist, political scientist, human rights activist and one of the young leaders: Nariman Celal.

Nariman Dzhelal, respected by all of us, and whom I know personally, did not leave the peninsula after 2014. Being in Crimea, he reported on events by calling them by their proper names. Media controlled by the occupiers were denied to him, so he used his own social networks and independent media, which are mainly located within the territory of Ukraine. He talked about every search, kidnapping, and other violations of the rights of the indigenous people of Crimea and discrimination that the Crimean Tatars experienced. He tried to help the families of political prisoners. He actively participated on international platforms, talking about systematic searches in the homes of Crimean Tatars and about the fate of illegally convicted compatriots. He was a voice that was not afraid to speak the truth, even if he was repeatedly warned and asked to be quiet.

In September last year, in order to silence and isolate him from society, first of all from his people, Nariman Celal was detained, accused of sabotage. Now he is in a pre-trial detention center. They want to put him in prison for fifteen years. The accusation is based soley on the testimony of hidden witnesses, there is not a single piece of evidence.

At that time, the Crimean media, controlled by the invaders, on the day of Nariman's detention, without trial or investigation, called him a saboteur, as if his guilt had already been proven.

At the same time, Russian politicians, public figures, and bloggers on television on the YouTube platform justify the deportation and genocide of the Crimean Tatars, justify the persecution of representatives of our people and systematically humiliate and insult us, yet the Russian law enforcement agencies that de facto control Crimea do not react to this.

They say no one is responsible for hate speech, while the Crimean Tatars are being insulted on a national basis for false materials in the media and comments on social networks.

Propaganda media outlets continue to use the terms 'extremists' and 'terrorists' in relation to the Crimean Tatars. All because our people do not recognize the occupation of Crimea and do not recognize the occupying regime and continue the non-violent struggle. The whole civilized world is in solidarity with us. This irritates the occupiers and the media controlled by them.

"Crimean Tatar extremists are raising the Crimean issue against the backdrop of the conflict in Donbas", "Why are Crimean Tatar radicals fighting for Crimea, while it is getting further and further from Ukraine", "Why has it not been possible to "clean up" the radical Crimean Tatar underground in 5 years on the peninsula?"—such headlines are full of propaganda media in Crimea and in Russia as well. This is all within the framework of the Russian state information policy.

Dear colleagues, we have all gathered here to discuss the influence of Russian propaganda, how it poisons people's minds. I, as a representative of the indigenous Crimean Tatar people, wonder—who will be held responsible and when will they be held responsible for insulting my people, my feelings? Why is the Russian media, without trial or investigation, allowed to call my people extremists and terrorists? They are replicating this all over the world in order to discredit our people. How long will I be humiliated in my native land?

After 2014, Ukrainian and international independent information resources were blocked in Crimea. It is not possible to open any information portal to read or see the true picture of what is happening in Ukraine and in the world. This is done on purpose to deprive people of the truth, of information, so that people remain under the full influence of the propaganda machine and become hostages of their lies and untruths.

Crimea has become a peninsula of fear, and madness; an information ghetto. On my native peninsula, propaganda media actively create the image of the Crimean Tatars as terrorists and extremists, and Ukrainians are shown as nationalists and Nazis. Against this background, history is being rewritten—by destroying the Crimean Tatar ethnic group, they creating a new myth about Russian Crimea.

Propaganda media only contribute to this, inciting and creating hate speech. YouTube and other international platforms are only used by them to spread lies. Only by blocking the propaganda media machine on these platforms, we can deprive them of the ability to poison the minds of people in Russia, in the territories it occupies, and in other countries.

The current Russian regime is held together by intimidation, lies, and propaganda. We must end this.

WAR
MENTALITY/DIGITALITY

"YOU MAY NOT BE INTERESTED IN CYBERWAR, BUT CYBERWAR IS INTERESTED IN YOU."

INTERVIEW WITH SVITLANA MATVIYENKO BY GEERT LOVINK

Early July 2022. Four months into her diary project Svitlana writes me: "Sirens are here again—since 3 am, they say we can't ignore sirens anymore, since Russia changed the tactics on June 26 and is now targeting cities; so I am sitting on the floor in the corridor, with my computer and my emergency backpack, waiting until the siren is canceled and I can go to sleep." Already before the Russian invasion started, I contacted the Canadian media theorist Svitlana Matviyenko to ask her how she was estimating the large-scale Russian exercises and the build-up at the border. On February 21 she responded: "I have been writing a diary since early January. I call it *Dispatches from the Place of Imminence*, in which I am trying to reflect on the situation, and particularly, the cyber warfare side of it. Some of this material can be already turned into texts for publication." This is how the Ukraine blog on the Institute of Network Cultures website was born.[1] On the day of the invasion she wrote me, in telegram style: "Banks are not working. ATMs give very limited cash (abt 35$), but you need cash everywhere now. All basic meds and drinking water are gone at the stores. But I was able to buy one remaining power bank in town. Russians occupied Chernobyl." On February 25, we published her first and a dozen entries would follow. The series will continue, copy-edited by London-based colleague and long-term INC collaborator Michael Dieter, who's also a member of the Tactical Media Room.

While Svitlana and I got to know each other online a decade earlier and met a few times here and there, we started working together in late October 2019, in Kyiv, when she invited me to participate in a conference of the Kyiv Biennale she organized, in collaboration with the Visual Culture Research Center. At the time, the war in the Donbas was already going on for a good five years with over ten thousand deaths— their photos scattered in makeshift memorials on streets and inside buildings. With the overall theme *Black Cloud,* the symposium was called *Communicative Militarism* and carried the slogan "You may not be interested in cyberwar, but cyberwar is interested in you." The description started off with the observation that "cyberwar, and overall militarisation of online communication, often remains overlooked in current discussions on surveillance capitalism, biased algorithms, and unjust infrastructures, including those of the internet." And concludes: "No matter what form it takes—subtle molding of users' sense of reality, leaking, hacking or direct attacks on critical infrastructure, cyberwar is fully integrated in the systemic operations of surveillance capitalism by sustaining crisis as a driving force of neoliberal economy and warfare spelled out far beyond the typical domains of war."

---

1   *Institute of Network Cultures: Dispatches from the Place of Imminence*, (2022), Institute of Network Cultures, https://networkcultures.org/blog/category/ukraine/.

In the following email exchange I have tried to cover both the wider context of the diary and address personal curiosities and concerns I had over past months as commissioning editor of the dispatches.

Geert Lovink: Reading your dispatches I have often tried to imagine the environment in which you have been writing: a table with a view, in a small town, a house perhaps, with a garden, not far from a Soviet-style block of flats, not unlike the Bukovina region that I know; a green and lush, sleepy 19th century landscape where time stands still, with deep marks of the Soviet era. For sure, I am romanticizing. Can you still see the ordinary in the midst of all the violent, depressing war news?

Svitlana Matviyenko: It's true, the urban landscape of my town, Kamyanets-Podilsky, which is as old as Amsterdam, is complex and layered. From my window on the top floor of the tallest building in town, I see the 13th century castle, the Old Fortress, built on the island surrounded by the river Smotrych, and I see the 19thn century architecture mixed with Soviet-era buildings as well as several ridiculous private houses of the local rich—I call them 'architectural porno' for their desperate effort to simulate medieval castles and churches.

But the fields and villages around town that spread kilometers and kilometers towards the horizon that I observe from my balcony, really make it easy to overlook the occasional ugliness by focusing on the magnificent ancient landscape of Podilsky Tovtry. 'Tovtry' is the local name of a rocky arc-shaped ridge, a barrier reef from the Miocene Sea that stretches parallel to the ancient coastal line, since this land is the bottom of that ancient sea. If you travel one hour south-east from my town towards Kytaihorod and the abandoned villages nearby, there is a place known to all geologists of the world: you encounter an unprecedented number of visible layers of geological periods—nine, if I remember correctly, with their typical fossils all open for you to observe and touch as you walk along the 541-million-year naturally formed 'road' down the valley, where in the 1940s my father used to walk their cow to graze, when he, not even a 10-year old boy, had to work nights and days like other Soviet peasant children after WWII to survive, which prevented him from finishing elementary school.

Historically, the town has been the nexus of different cultures and ethnicities—Ukrainian, Jewish, Armenian, Turkish, Polish, and Russian. Although it was not exactly a peaceful coexistence at all times, these people demonstrated an impressive appreciation for each other's cultural artefacts that were not erased or demolished, but carefully preserved. Where else will you see, for example, a catholic cathedral with an attached minaret and the statue of Virgin Mary on its top? That's Kamyanets.

War really makes your optic hyper-sensitive to the ordinary and to the everyday surrounding overall. While any war, probably, has this effect, this current conflict has revealed the shocking urge for the erasure of people and culture on the part of our invaders, when everything that survived World War I and II is now being demolished and destroyed in the centre and south-east of the country. There is a new sense of ultimate fragility of all life and non-life forms, including that 541-million-year old stony landscape...

GL: You are neither a war reporter on the ground, nor a Western opinion maker. You have become a North-American media theorist, academic, teacher. How would you describe your role? I read your dispatches as a hybrid genre between political analysis, media theory and a personal diary. By the way, I always wanted to ask you: is there an actual diary? You make notes first, you told me. Lately someone asked if the entries were written in Ukrainian or Russian. I know they are written by you directly in English, but is there an issue of language for you in this case?

SM: This *is* an actual diary, but there are still unused drafts and many undeveloped notes that will join the text when it becomes a book. I had to leave some things out. Sometimes, it was the matter of pressing time. You remember, probably, that I used to send the dispatches every several days, and I was not able to include and develop everything that I noted. A month into the war, I became part of some initiatives of which I still cannot speak on record or publicly since it would put some people at risk. Then, of course, just like we cannot photograph local infrastructures of defence or strategic objects, we cannot talk about some details or circumstances, which I keep writing about in my notes. Other events of the war are admittedly very hard to evaluate either due to a lack of information or, on the contrary, due to their overwhelmingly heated or distorted perception.

I do touch upon some of the controversial topics in my text, but in some cases I need more time myself to process what is happening. All these notes will make it to the planned book version, as I think—or I really hope—it would be possible to reveal many incredible details of pride and disappointment in about half a year or so from now, when the manuscript goes to the press; I have started reworking the early entries already. This may look like an unusual way of writing a diary, but then maybe it has to do with the fact that it is a war dairy, with its temporal folds that will fully open to the reader with a certain delay. In this sense, writing a war diary is a very particular practice, I suppose.

I write this diary in English. Despite the occasional grammar issues and my thick accent, this is the language that, at this point of my life, gives shape to my thoughts faster than other languages, including my both native languages—Ukrainian and Russian. I speak Ukrainian with all my friends and colleagues, and will with my father, who speaks 'Surzhyk', a local dialect that combines Ukrainian, Russian, and other words that are typical only for this region; I speak Russian with my mother; and I speak only English with my sister who lives in Chicago, and who speaks Russian with both of my parents. So, it's complicated.

GL: During Covid, while you were in the south-west of Ukraine, you continued your teaching commitments online, like most of us, via Zoom and Teams. This is a part of your life and work you have not yet written about in the dispatches. Can you share some of your insights with us on this? Vancouver is literally on the other side of the globe. During the war period you spent a considerable amount of time there, virtual, mentally, workwise.

SM: It's true. Like everyone, I began teaching online in March 2020 due to the Covid pandemic at the beginning of the quarantine. In February 2021, I went to Ukraine, after almost two years of not being able to see my 85-year old parents, which was hard for me as they both were not feeling well, and then my mother broke her spine on the third day I got to my hometown. So, I continued online teaching from a different time zone with a 10-hour difference from my university. Then, by the end of summer 2021, I discovered I was sick and needed treatment, which I immediately began in Ukraine, because by then I already lost my Canadian health care plan, so my university approved a prolonged stay until Spring 2022. In February 2022, however, the Russian invasion brought the war regime on top of all the 'unusual circumstances.'

When we started using Zoom, in spring 2020, with my colleagues at the School of Communication, we were rather concerned about the adoption of Zoom by our and other universities, due to many security and privacy problems that had been found in how this platform operated, including poor encryption, tracking attendees of the meetings and more. Many of us experimented with other platforms, but I am not sure this is still the case. While in Vancouver, like many, I remember I often experienced so-called 'Zoom fatigue,' but I did not feel any of that in Ukraine: I guess, amidst everything going on with my family and in my country, the hierarchy of risks changes your attitude and perception. That is how bad tech sinks into our lives, in the circumstances of threats and risks. In February and March of 2022, when the telecommunication infrastructure was damaged by shelling and I lost the possibility of using video or voice, I had to quickly redesign my graduate seminar to adjust to the circumstances by moving to text communication via Google Docs. The impact of the last two and a half years of Covid and the war has only started showing up—my vision, of course, got much worse (I've changed my glasses twice already); my short-term memory fails spectacularly and in the strangest ways: I may 'forget' for whom I am writing an article while in the process of writing it, and need to scroll up to the text's title to remind myself of the details.

Teaching during the war has been more challenging for me content-wise. I had several difficult moments when I lost sense of what I was doing and why—and the waves of depression keep returning more regularly now, after the war has entered a slow grind, which also tells me it may become endless. Teaching the works of thinkers who, at this moment, call your country to surrender and cede the territories to the imperialist state has been, to put it mildly, a devastating experience of disorientation and disappointment, undermining the core of my being. It feels like we are back in the 18th century and all the volumes of post- and decolonial thought are evaporating as we speak.

GL: You must have thought about this. How would you write the additional chapter on the 2022 Russian invasion of Ukraine if your 2019 book *Cyberwar and Revolution: Digital Subterfuge in Global Capitalism* that you co-authored with Nick Dyer-Witheford would have a second edition? How do you see this war in light of the cyberwarfare tactics that you described in that book? There is fake news, but also drones and occasional news of Russian cyber-attacks. However, if I think of comparisons, it is Putin's Syria strategy that comes to mind: brutal urban destruction Aleppo-style, not sophisticated hacks, or am I wrong here?

SM: Several years back, Nick and I were often told, with implied criticism, that our term 'cyberwar' and the emphasis on 'war' seemed blown out of proportions. "War involves bloodshed," we were told. But we emphasized that cyberwar is both 'cyber' and 'kinetic,' morphing and oscillating between these two poles, where, in a blink of an eye, it becomes total bloodshed, mobilizing populations within the complex assemblages of communicative militarism, where commercial platforms are merged with military technology and techniques of social engineering and psyops. Its temporality is defined by both brisk tactics and long-term strategies, like those implemented by *Russia Today*, for example, which aim to shape useful audiences across the world, to build their trust by parasiting, like John Carpenter's *The Thing*, all progressive concerns and agendas so that people are tricked into thinking this channel indeed shares their values, while methodically planting the idea that Ukraine is ultra-nationalist through and through, and, therefore, is a threatening fake state—a very comforting idea, to be honest, for the left and liberals who proved incapable of fighting far-right groups in their own countries: Ukraine has become a realm of outsourced failures for all. It is also a phantasmatic playground, the very existence of which allowed many in the world to stage their own economic and political fantasies, and score points. So, I guess, it could be interesting to engage again in the psychoanalytic discussion of these 'structures' that not only take to the streets, but also go to war.

Another theme that we addressed rather briefly in the book, and that certainly demands an extensive discussion now, is the nuclear dimension of this war, which reveals the disturbing imperial legacies from Soviet and pre-Soviet 'external' and 'internal' colonial practices in the current Russian energy terrorism. Nuclear cyberwar is not just about the infamous red button, but the weaponization of the physical atomic energy infrastructure and its computational components by disconnecting nuclear plants from the international monitoring systems.

Lastly, this eight-year war reveals itself as the first war seen by the world spectator almost in real time. It does not mean, however, that this war is fully transparent or observable for a human eye. Probably on the contrary. With all the available immediacy by means of AI and OSINT, weaponized and used for targeting, and with all the Maxar-powered optics, this is certainly an a-human war in several ways: it operates at machinic speeds—either too fast and too slow—by excommunication, reification, resourcification, and elimination of the user—a civilian or a soldier.

GL: You've described the live Azovstal resistance broadcast as an unprecedented cyberwar event. Can you take us back? What exactly happened there?

SM: This relates to my previous point about the war being open to real-time observation. Indeed, the case of the 84-day Azovstal steel plant resistance was extraordinary for different reasons. Azovstal was fully blockaded by Russian forces on April 10th, and Ukrainian soldiers with many civilians were locked underground without water, food, meds, and ammunition. Many wounded lost their limbs or died due to the lack or absence of antibiotics. The conditions there were terrifying. Several attempts—seven, they now say—to deliver all these necessary things to Azovstal by helicopter failed one after another, with the Ukrainian side losing both pilots and helicopters altogether. At the same time, the defenders were able to video-[2] and

---

2   *Фортеця Маріуполь. Останній день на Азовсталі.* (2022, May 21). [Video]. YouTube. https://www. youtube.com/watch?v=azldlmJUolc.

photo-document[3] their life underground, as Dmytro Kozatsky did, showing the insides of the legendary 'Fortress Mariupol' one day before the extraction (which, however, would eventually turn into straightforward captivity in the territory of the grey area of the so-called DNR) and to continue communicating not only with their commanding officers and journalists, but with the broader world by posting appeals and even by holding international live press conferences in English from underground while Russian forces bombarded the Azovstal territory with artillery and aircraft.[4]

GL: One of the most significant developments in the Western/US internet context during the Russian invasion of Ukraine has been Elon Musk's attempt to take over Twitter. How did people in Ukraine perceive the turmoil this caused? Twitter may be a mid-sized social network in terms of users, yet it plays an important role in terms of agenda-setting for the Western news. Would you say that Telegram is playing a similar role?

SM: Unless I missed something, there was no concern whatsoever regarding Musk's attempt to take over Twitter. Partly because neither the Ukrainian government nor Ukrainian users are particularly concerned about the corporate politics of social media platforms. Before the invasion in February, the government had been reimagining itself using Silicon Valley style rhetoric and logic of start-up culture ala "the state in a smartphone" (держава в смартфоні). Also, the most popular platforms are Facebook, YouTube, Instagram, Telegram and only then Twitter, followed only by the blocked Russian platforms Vkontakte and Odnoklassniki. The ideas of deregulation are usually met with excitement, unlike the ideas of regulation. In my casual conversations with people about Musk, the move towards deregulating Twitter and what it would mean, for example, for Russian disinformation campaigns, people usually reacted by dismissing my arguments by saying "it cannot be so," or "Musk knows what he is doing." Musk is a hero in Ukraine. This perception has been shaped earlier, when his biography by Ashlee Vance was translated, published, and widely read in Ukraine. From what I heard it was a bestseller, then his ongoing confrontation with Director General of Roscosmos Dmitry Rogozin certainly added to his popularity, and, of course, his overall story of 'successful success.' But still, all this is nothing in comparison to Musk's support for Ukraine over the last several months.

First of all, the immediacy of his reaction was spectacular. Vice Prime Minister of Ukraine and Minister of Digital Transformation Mykhailo Fedorov tweeted to Musk on February 26th, and on February 28th, the first Starlink terminals were in Ukraine. Here, as always, a war is the context for setting new precedents in logistics. The use of the Starlink satellite system in the context of war was also an unprecedented learning and testing experience. The presence of Starlink in Ukraine matters a lot. The government and military have both relied on these encrypted satellites. The Ukrainian drones operate via

3   *Photo full size.* (2022). Google Drive. https://drive.google.com/drive/folders/1efz3M_
     yHIJG6EYB57J9Di8V85MJco51l.
4   Official appeal of Azov commander, the major Denis Prokopenko, to the world community. (2022,
     March 7). [Video]. YouTube. https://www.youtube.com/watch?v=ajKa2X_-Q74.
     Цензор.НЕТ | Необхідно виконати дію. (2022, May 8). censor.net. https://censor.net/en/video_
     news/3339916/press_conference_with_azovstal_defenders_in_mariupol_ukraine_video.

Starlink connections, whose encryption seems rather resilient having survived massive cyberattacks from Russia, while SpaceX keeps rewriting the code. In fact, the Ukrainian troops in the Azovstal steel plant were able to maintain contact with their commanders and conduct live video interviews with journalists, as I mentioned above, because they had a Starlink system in the blockaded steel plant. The connection was stable there until the final hours of the soldiers' presence at the plant and this is despite Russia's aggressive radio-electric warfare tools that have been used extensively in this war. So Starlink constitutes an important layer in this complex cyberwar assemblage. Using it, however, posits some threats, as it happens, because these transmissions can be triangulated and targeted, as John Scott-Railton noted, given the history of Russia targeting satellite communications in several previous military involvements.[5]

It was rather telling when Serhiy Volynskyi, commander of Ukraine's 36th Separate Marine Brigade, also blockaded at Azovstal, appealed to Musk for help asking to rescue soldiers by means of the extraction procedure from the besieged plant in a tweet on May 12th. "People say you come from another planet to teach people to believe in the impossible. Our planets are next to each other, as I live where it is nearly impossible to survive. Help us get out of Azovstal to a mediating country. If not you, then who? Give me a hint," he wrote. It is incredibly painful to read these words, a gesture of despair directed to someone who in the imagination of many embodies the Good.

GL: You have often been to the Chernobyl Zone, already many years ago. You have done research there and recently got a Canadian grant to continue that work on the ground. How do you look at that topic, that place, in light of the war? And what are your research plans at the moment?

SM: By now, I've got already two Canadian research grants for the projects *Chernobyl Science* and *Border as Medium: A Case of the Chernobyl Zone*, and I am launching the work here as I will stay in Ukraine for another year. It will be tricky, as the access to the Zone is extremely restricted now, but I am working on obtaining the pass. Parts of the Zone are mined, but the military have been working on eliminating them for quite some time. I've been always extremely careful on my field trips, the safety rules are pretty much the same—no wandering off route, no touching objects, no eating outside, long sleeves and no shorts, even in heat, no smoking, no interaction with wild animals. The radiation level remains safe. I have an incredible team of people here who spent over twenty years researching and monitoring the Zone who were first to get back to their offices and labs after the Russian troops withdrew. I also have a broad network of people living inside and immediately outside the Chernobyl Zone. Several bridges on the way to Chernobyl are now demolished, so it also posits a certain difficulty. One of my projects was supposed to be about the border infrastructure, which is non-existent now. At the same time, there are so many new questions and perspectives opening up in relation to the recent occupation, one of which is again about the contours of the Chernobyl Zone, given its distributed

5   Scott-Railton, J. (2022, February 27). *John Scott-Railton on starlink* [Tweet with image]. Twitter. https://twitter.com/jsrailton/status/1497745011932286979.

territoriality. 2022 was certainly the most important year for Chernobyl Zone history after 1986, as it revealed both imperial and colonial legacies of the Soviet Union that so powerfully came forward, carried forth by the forces of the Russian Federation through the Chernobyl Zone, in the first days of the invasion.

DIGITAL LEVIATHAN AND HIS NUCLEAR TAIL: NOTES ON BODY AND THE EARTH IN THE STATE OF WAR

OLEXII KUCHANSKYI

This text was originally published by Your Art. *Translated by Teta Tsybulnyk, Kyiv-based artist, ruïns collective. The English version was then published on e-flux. Here the text is republished with the author's consent.*

"By state of war I mean state in the sense that physicists or chemists think about states of matter. Every state of matter is an order, and despite that order, every state of matter has some elements of other states," writes political theorist and philosopher Jairus Grove.[1] 'World,' 'life,' 'reality,' 'earth,' and 'body' are the categories whose established interrelations have been unsettled by the state of war.

Watching the war (a film found online), 2018.

---

1   Grove, J. V. (2019). *Savage Ecology: War and Geopolitics at the End of the World.* Duke University Press, 60.

The Deadly Preemption

In 2022, after centuries of molting, the Hobbesian Leviathan is covered with scales that neither the authors of medieval engravings nor the political philosophers of the 17th century could have envisioned. The huge and eerie shell of this monster consists of millions of screens and radars—its armor and weapons, its camouflage and tools of intimidation. Nowadays, in the current state of war, multitudes of bodies literally fear, hope, tremble, seek opportunities to move to a temporarily safer place, head to work or to a military recruitment office—in short, they vibrate—together with these screens, which fabricate both facts and emotions, like sincerity and fear. The monster also unleashes the sound of sirens that regulate the bodily rhythms of those who are trapped in the warzone: sleep, movement, the contractions of muscles, and the secretion of gastric juice out of horror. All of this constitutes just a few millimeters on this huge monster's scaly skin.

Each movement of his limbs provokes terabytes of panic, spasms, and hundreds of deaths. This must be the creature that Manuel DeLanda, political theorist and researcher of contemporary wars, described back in the 1990s, noting the transferring of control from humans to software systems—not just digital technologies but human-machine systems operated by both men and machines.[2] According to another author, Canadian philosopher Brian Massumi, contemporary regimes rely more than ever on such fusions, particularly between the procedures of representative democracy, information technologies (media), and the military sphere. Massumi claims that social tension reached its boiling point after the September 11th attacks—the destruction of the Twin Towers in Manhattan carried out by al-Qaeda members.[3]

2   DeLanda, M. (1992). *War in the Age of Intelligent Machines.* Zone Books, 167–71.
3   Massumi, B. (2015). *Ontopower: War, Powers, and the State of Perception.* Duke University Press Books.

The Antichrist sits on Leviathan. An illustration from Liber Floridus, a medieval encyclopedia compiled by Lambert of Saint-Omer, 1120. Wikimedia Commons.

This event led the administration of the US president George W. Bush to develop measures aimed at the 'preemption' of undesirable events, most of which were labelled with the well-known but incomprehensible term 'terrorism.' The term is incomprehensible, explains Massumi, because it has an unstable meaning: it refers not to actual but potential phenomena and events, which have nowadays become the objects of management. Media messages, among other things, are a crucial weapon of preemption—they 'visualize' the newly invented threat and provoke fear, which is a powerful political tool. They take root in the whirlpool of political and social events, in the affective states and behaviors of the population, even though they can only attest to the probable.[4]

---

4   Massumi, B. (2015). *Ontopower: War, Powers, and the State of Perception.* Duke University Press Books.

The way the Russian government rationalizes its invasion of Ukraine, and more broadly, Putin's statements about 'extremism' and the threat from NATO, together prove that the doctrine of preemption has now found its way to Russia too. The preemption of constructed threats ('peacekeeping') and preventive measures to outmaneuver other geopolitical actors determine tens of millions of actual destinies.[5] Massumi wrote about 'ontopower'; now it makes sense to speak of 'ontowar'—the destruction of what is alive in order to prevent what is possible. How else can we understand the fact that 'peacekeeping' implies the use of weapons and the targeted killing of civilians? Hiding in bomb shelters, we watch this fatal poker game, becoming 'instruments' and at the same time victims of Russia's 'bluff.' But despite all the manipulations and tricks, the rules of the game involve a 'kinetic' network of preemptions where every step is either an amicable gesture or a threat. It is a game that is played at the cost of thousands of lives.

17-07-2015 21:07:54
Avdeevka

эта война начата для того, чтобы быть увиденой

P290 ¦ T06   Z001

Watching the War (a film found online), 2018.

This War Began in Order To Be Seen

Is it possible to imagine the interplay between the real and the probable as something different than a dance of the scaly beast—the bloody 'manager' of social fears and geopolitical decisions? It might be worth looking at some attempts at imagining this that come from a

---

5   Massumi's theory doesn't offer an exhaustive explanation of current political events. But, in my opinion, it helps us understand why some political (in the widest sense) processes get a certain expression. After all, this theory of power is not limited to explaining the actions of the state apparatus, which makes it worth our attention as 'the population.'

time before the escalation of the war in Ukraine—from the time of its origins, during the hostilities in Donbas in 2014–22. One of the most remarkable attempts of this kind was 'Watching the war (a film found online) (2018)'. This work was created by 443 anonymous videographers who shared their amateur mobile phone footage on social media. The footage was then edited by an anonymous film editor (or a collective). All this video documentation of the war in Eastern Ukraine was made by its immediate witnesses from 2014 to 2018. There are no television graphics, no sensational talking heads, no prophecies by experts. Only five and a quarter hours of raw video evidence of war. Some fragments of the film include intertitles with brief commentary. One of them states, "the war began in order to be seen." Amidst the 'war of preemption' that the Russian Federation legitimizes with its televised content, and the (justifiably) regulated visual regime in Ukraine, this statement is truer than ever before.

Something between AI and Nuclear

Svitlana Matviyenko, co-author of the book 'Cyberwar and Revolution', recently wrote: "The war tension oscillates between two poles these seven days—AI and nuclear."[6] The internet, deepfakes, automated alert systems (sirens), and occupied nuclear power stations are the new attributes of war. Yet, just a few weeks ago, it was impossible to imagine how much could transpire between those poles: murders, artillery shelling, the siege of Mariupol, missile attacks on residential areas, nights in the metro, sirens, sirens, sirens, sirens, a friend I haven't been able to contact for a week now, a cruise missile destroying my favorite Czechoslovakian tea set that I got from grandma along with five floors of the building, bombings of kindergartens, boarding schools, and maternity hospitals, green corridors—red rooms, sirens and bombings, thev sixteenth day—slept-through sirens and carried-out bombings, a fire at the biggest nuclear power station in Europe, it's cold—where to get warm clothes?, the rape and abduction of women, uncontrolled fear for the life of your beloved, silence about those killed—out of impossibility, inadequacy, or inability to talk about it?

This is exactly the case when testimonies are much more eloquent than any interpretation of them. They manifest why the war must be stopped and never happen again, undermining cynical media chatter about strategies and preemption.

My friend, anarchist and art scholar, who joined the Territorial Defense Forces:

> Here's how I am: night duty is a very special state of mind. Everything around me becomes a meditation. Every splash of water, every movement of the trees. You try to be on guard all the time and all your memories, thoughts, and identifications get blurred as if out of focus—there is just you, your gun, the guys, and the territory. One commander says that the most fucked-up guarding happens in autumn, when the leaves fall from the trees—it sounds as if someone is walking around you. It's interesting to imagine that, but I wouldn't want to experience it.

---

6   Matviyenko, S. (2022, March 5). *Dispatches from the Place of Imminence, part 3*. Institute of Network Cultures. https://networkcultures.org/blog/2022/03/05/dispatches-from-the-place-of-imminence-by-svitlana-matviyenko-part-3/.

During small breaks, we warmed ourselves in the dugout and exchanged a few words. Seeing a crying child showing through the stitches of a tough masculine commander feels like having a mixer in your stomach. After this, one could space out staring at the grass really long. A sudden bus at high speed during the curfew, 'ready' command, position, stock, aim. It turns out to be the bus carrying morning-shift workers. Back to smoking.

At dawn, Dima and I talked about cinema. Dima believes that cinema is inferior to literature as a means of expression because you spend much more time with a book than a film. It's a really interesting point, something to dig into. I studied at the department of art theory & history and I never thought of it. Dima served in the military after school and worked at the factory all his life. He listens to rap, smokes pot, and tries to have fun. He is thirty-eight, his child was born last year. He likes Wong Kar-wai and is a fan of Asian cinema in general. Dima communicates by quoting Omar Khayyam, Confucius, and other awesome guys.

As it was getting dark, the cop began to talk about Maidan. My platoon commander turned out to be an ex-cop. Talks about coup d'états, power, and theft. Fishermen, factory workers, former patrolmen, pensioners, junkies, alcoholics, contract soldiers from urban villages and regional centers. It's like interviewing people who could easily be labeled 'the salt of the earth,' but then the shift ends, civilian life rapidly breaks in, and 'common sense' reminds you that everything is not so clear-cut and it shouldn't be seen as black and white. No cigarettes in shops, endless queues for free chicken from the humanitarian aid distribution points. I inhale the last puff and drift off. Soon there should be news from another city; maybe the guys can take me to a new platoon of their military unit. I wake up late in the evening, waiting for the moment when my parents fall asleep. Now I'm sitting and writing this improvised report. Life goes on and that's beautiful.

My friend Asia Bazdyrieva, researcher and member of the Geocinema collective, in her notes about the war: "I could no longer talk, I simply howled. Not wept, but howled like an animal. There was a break between the world and reality, and I was thrown on this side."[7]

A howl and a break, 'a mixer in the stomach'—this is something bigger than 'I,' a separate personality with its own experiences.

Autonomous Weapons and Geosomatocide

'Autonomous weapons' (unmanned tanks, cruise missiles, anti-aircraft missiles, anti-missile satellites) and cyberattacks have hardly proven to be the means of more humane wars with minimal losses. Quite the contrary: as part of the military and police formation of Putinism,

---

7   Письмо из Украины: Семь дней. (2022, March 3). Syg.Ma. https://syg.ma/@asia-bazdyrieva/pismo-iz-ukrainy-siem-dniei.

they have turned civilians' bodies into targets of 'functional damage.' Artist Dana Kavelina, who made the film 'Letter to a Turtledove,' once pointed out that bodies, first and foremost female ones, are the media for messages sent by the aggressor. Again: this "war began in order to be seen."

Among the multiple reasons to label Putinism as fascism, one is that both are practical incarnations of drastic futurist reveries. These reveries extol technology and destruction, and evince a hatred for the body. But Putinism incorporates something that the futurists lacked: neoliberal capitalism as the condition for the corruption of the international organizations that should have guaranteed peace.

This will to annihilate allows us to highlight something that connects AI and nuclear power: the body, but not as an individual human organism, rather as a network of 'my' relationships and interactions, as a tension between the individual and its environment. In this sense, a conglomeration of selves united by a common territory form a multiple body—a shared membrane where fear, pain, and hope spread from Mariupol, Kharkiv, and Kherson to Lviv and Uzhhorod, and now also to Warsaw, Krakow, Berlin, and Bucharest, and back. It is important to note that when it comes to the geopolitical decisions of both Russia and the international organizations trying to preserve peace for the sake of "humanity," the Ukrainian bodies are not entirely human. First and foremost, we are quantitative indicators; that is, we are a human shield for Europe, and we are targets on a map for the Russian Federation, since human rights are clearly the rights of Western humans only. The Ukrainian body is at best the object of humanitarian aid, but not of ius humanitatis.[8]

Geo in 'geopolitics' and 'geography' has regained its literal meaning. In Greek, *geo* is the earth. Nowadays in Ukraine there is nothing more unstable than the territory, but at the same time nothing more tangible than the earth. Geosomatic community. The war in Ukraine is geosomatocide: the destruction of bodies, the devastation of the earth, and a nuclear threat hanging over Europe. Military aggression as a response to what might have happened seeps into bodies along with air and water, grows into green zones, leaves residential areas in ruins, and takes hundreds of lives daily. Recall the quote from Jairus Grove: "By state of war I mean state in the sense that physicists or chemists think about states of matter." The perverse epistemic software of the capitalist West and of Putin's extractivist patriarchal regime cannot register the magnitude of the losses taking place: the earth, whose abstraction is territory, and bodies, whose abstraction is population numbers.

According to a perverse capitalist reason, the losses for actors and observers are totally different. Someone risks their bank account numbers, even though these numbers are so huge that it's impossible to convert them into any tangible human value. On the other hand, except for radar 'threats' and arithmetic indicators, this game means scorched earth, destroyed buildings, interrupted future, and lost lives. Military processes, both actual and potential, are embedded into bodies and landscapes—as physical and chemical reactions provoked by high-tech weapons, as mass migrations of bodies around the planet, as clouds

---

8   Human rights.

of dust that can't settle between explosions and shellings, as mutilated bodies and fractured lives. This situation would look totally hopeless if the Global West hadn't already faced the organized political rebellion of bodies and the earth—decolonial and ecofeminist groups, leftists against the extractivist appetites of capitalism, and cooperated movements of the displaced who are sick of being 'quantified.'

Yet it is complicated to answer the question of how a whole neighboring country has become an automated weapon of mass destruction that acts not only against its own population but also against the logic of capital accumulation. This is exactly the reason to think of the old character from political theology tales—Leviathan.

Tentative Conclusions

The past sixteen days testify to something important. Back in the 17th century, philosopher Baruch Spinoza, in his unfinished *Tractatus Politicus* (1677), proposed a distinction between *potestas*, or power in the legal sense, and *potentia multitudinis*, the potency of multitudes united by a common political goal.[9] Right now, potentia multitudinis, witnessed in thousands of volunteer efforts and military operations, concentrates around its most powerful weapons—solidarity and hope. As such, they can't ensure safety, but they make it possible to keep up and even rekindle peace—one of the most fragile things in the world. And they make the digital Leviathan, with his nuclear tail, reconsider his plans.

---

9   Spinoza, B. (1670). *Tractatus Theologico-Politicus: Tractatus Politicus.*

I NOTICE THE EXTENSION

LERA MALCHENKO

This text was originally published on the Bündnis Internationaler Produktionshäuser website as part of the ::: VOICES ::: UKRAINE project in April 2022. Here, the text is republished with the author's consent.

'Mine has a long whistle. A howitzer projectile sounds almost like a mine, but there is less time for escape. "Grad" in good weather can be heard from afar. A tank. Its shot can be heard along with the hit. "Smerch" sounds like a take-off fighter.'

These are excerpts from popular advice on Ukrainian social networks. If you haven't been under fire yet, you're trying to remember, but in vain. Everything gets confused. However, when your city comes under fire, you just get this experience, the worst possible media experience, which is immediately embedded into everyday life.

Still from 'New information: The big diffusion theory' by fantastic little splash, 2017.

"The sounds of war are always reminiscent of the sounds of everyday life, the sounds of everyday life will forever resemble the sounds of war", Ukrainians Dima Tolkachov and Maria Matyashova wrote on Instagram.[1] They also wrote that various weapons may sound as if something was rumbling on the construction site, or neighbors were pushing furniture, or a garbage truck overturned a container, or a door slammed in the hallway. And vice versa.[2] The sounds of the city thus also become the sounds of war. When you go outside, after air raid

---

1   *Image.* (2022, March 6). Instagram. https://www.instagram.com/p/Caw2sHwN2DL/.
2   *Image.* (2022, March 3). Instagram. https://www.instagram.com/p/CapB7pptkfi/.

sirens, for example, to buy some food, your heart stops at a hum of a trolleybus, a barely audible electric car engine, or a small power station near a supermarket (*"When it appeared here, I didn't notice?"*). A phantom siren is heard everywhere. Weapons are suspected in all machinery. In the early days of the war, I was thinking about Ernst Junger's *The Glass Bees*.[3] His narrator is a retired cavalryman who went to war with his horse. He loved his horse, considered it the dearest creature with whom he shared the most horrible moments of his life on a battlefield. Two living creatures before the fear of death became one — the desire to live. And here the main character remembers this first in the history of mankind horror of meeting an inhuman, with the personification of war in a machine—a tank. This is the main thing I remember after reading *The Glass Bees*—the human and the animal horror of the machine which were merged into one, in this horror they were one. In the same way I'm afraid of 'Grad', 'Kalibr', 'Tochka U'—what else do they have? I find a quote from Junger:

"What was the meaning of this thunderous roar, when on the ground turtles of steel and serpents of iron rolled past, while in the sky triangles, arrows, and rockets shaped like fish, arranged themselves with lightning rapidity into ever-changing formations? Though the display was continual, in this silence and these shouts something evil, old as time, manifested itself in man, who is an out-smarter and a setter of traps."[4]

I feel more and more like this primitive man for whom danger is now everywhere. NATO has repeatedly refused to 'close the skies' over Ukraine. And the Ukrainian sky, full of Russian missiles, has become a prehistoric danger, almost an element: total and inevitable. Civilian objects, streets, squares are under fire. Civilization no longer promises to get rid of dangers. *"The sky is licensed, but not at my home"*,—Ukrainian designer Ujn3000 signs his work.[5]

3   Junger, E., & Sterling, B. (2000). *The Glass Bees (New York Review Books Classics)* (1st ed.). NYRB Classics.
4   Junger, E., & Sterling, B. (2000). *The Glass Bees (New York Review Books Classics)* (1st ed.). NYRB Classics.
5   *Image*. (2022, March 8). Instagram. *https://www.instagram.com/p/Ca1gReDtS_H/*.

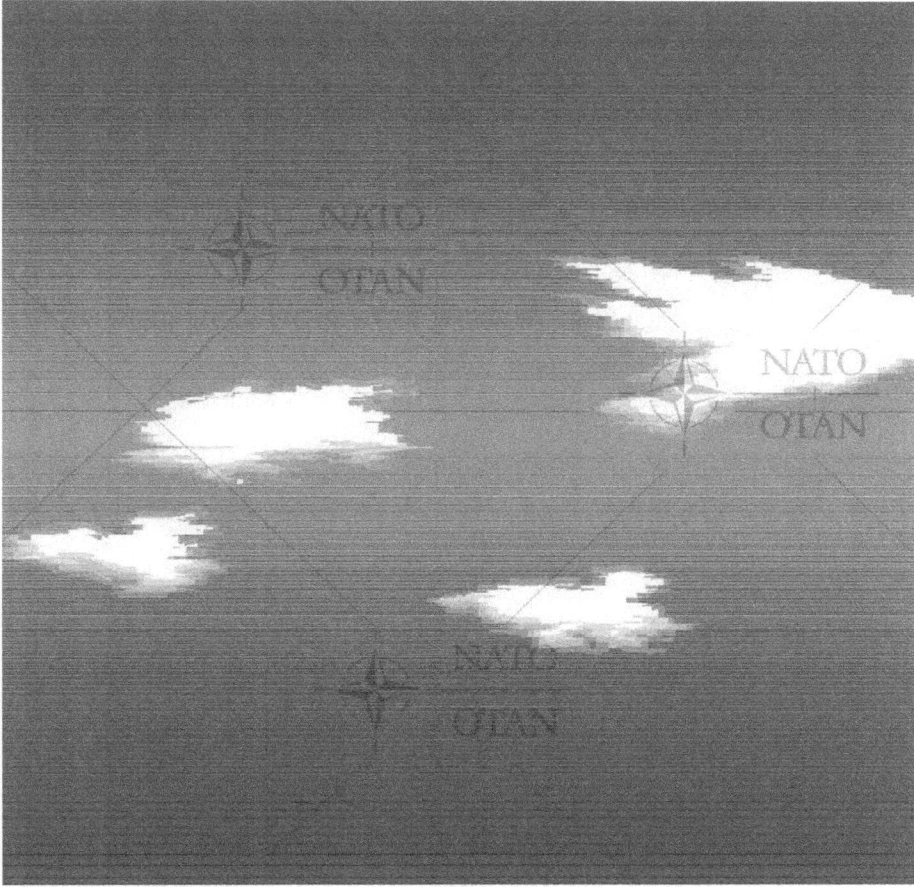

Illustration by Ujn3000.

I am now in a relatively safe western Ukrainian city, where air raid sirens are sounding, but there have been no bombings. I was taken in by friends of friends, M. and L., people whom I did not know before the war. But they sheltered me, and I still keep thinking about how I can thank them. I'm watching how M. plays 'Forbidden West,' the second part of 'Horizon,' which was published a week before the war.

Still from the 'Horizon: Forbidden West' videogame.

The protagonist Aloy, dressed as a fictional indigenous person, fights against powerful animalistic machines. Among other things, in her arsenal—'focus.' It is a device like a thermal imager, which is able to display information about all living and non-living things around: animals, resources and machines here find continuation in each other.

I notice that the sounds of Aloy's military gadgets disgust me. All experiences are rapidly shrinking, and then I feel the same rapid extension from within myself. I feel nauseous. For the first time, I noticed such an *extension* clearly and consciously on February 22, while watching Putin's hour-long gaslighting speech. It was a verbal annexation that felt like a real unauthorized aggressive invasion. Hatred, anger, denial of my existence was relayed in a symbolic space—in the Russian language. Then it was relayed by technological space—fiber optics made this threat possible. And then I felt like I had become a semiconductor of this hatred. I started to get the jitters. It was repeated on the 24th, with the sounds of explosions in my city, and then had been continuing sporadically for the next four days, during continuous reading of the news.

Then I felt this extension attack a week later, in an evacuation train. It was a sleeping railroad car with dimmed lights and draped windows, so as not to betray our movement. There were 12-15 people in each compartment, two or three on a shelf designed for one passenger. The children were crying, it was hot, the smell of hastily gathered food was spreading through the car and mixing with the smells of bodies. When the train left, the conductor turned off the lights completely, everything became dark. All that could be heard was the clatter of wheels and the squeak of the old car parts, the whispering of adults, the shushing at children for sudden loud cries, almost nothing could be seen. Men were allowed into the carriages only if there were seats left; mostly women and children were there. In this darkness, forced intimacy, suffocation, I felt us as one biological mass, *uterined* inside the train, which was rushed, then stood for a long time and creaked softly. Gender scenarios and mass mobilization have erased us all to basic functions in this event. I began to feel sick again and I went to the train vestibule, where I realized that if I do not begin to clearly feel the boundaries of my own body, I will experience dissociation. Focusing on breathing, squeezing one's hands and patting on the body returned the feeling of being an individual. I am separate from others, I am.

This frightening and at the same time encouraging collectivity has been a part of every Ukrainian's life for over a month now. Everything living and non-living is interrelated. And in the air raid sirens as well. The third part of Svitlana Matviyenko's diaries reads: "In moments like this, we are probably all united by the flight of the rocket, with most of us probably sharing the same affect. This is a profoundly cybernetic event of control and communication in the animal and the machine: an intermixing of complex heterogeneous systems at a huge scale."[6]

---

6   Matviyenko, S. (2022, March 5). *Dispatches from the Place of Imminence, part 3*. Institute of Network Cultures. https://networkcultures.org/blog/2022/03/05/dispatches-from-the-place-of-imminence-by-svitlana-matviyenko-part-3/.

Карта повітряних тривог
Дані станом на: 26 березня, 16:14 (31 день);
Автооновлення через 21 сек. Оновити

And even if sirens don't sound in a city at a particular time, everyone who follows the news sees it in telegram channels, several times for each city, and on the online air raid sirens map, which auto-updates every 21 seconds.

"The body as a network of 'my' relationships and interactions, the body as a tension between the individual and its environment. In this sense, heaping of individuals united by a common territory forms a united but multiple body - a common membrane, where fear, pain but also hope spread from Mariupol, Kharkiv and Kherson to Lviv and Uzhgorod, and now to Warsaw, Krakow, Berlin and Bucharest—and back", writes Olexii Kuchansky in the text 'Digital Leviathan and its nuclear tail: notes on the body and the ground in a martial law'.[7] Following the withdrawal of Russian troops from the Kyiv region and the distribution of photos and videos of the bodies of killed and tortured civilian Ukrainians left on the streets and basements, the pain escalated, own—multiplied by the collective, had become unbearable, but it was impossible to get through it alone. Moving and still images that violate Instagram rules have flooded the

---

7   See Olexii Kuchanskyi's text in this publication prior to this text.

feeds. Algorithms automatically had found content inappropriate, #bucha #buchamassacre tags are blocked. The company unblocked them in a day, but Ukrainian feeds continued to be blurred. Ukrainians retranslated the terror, but also tried to convey to the outside world what had happened. Blur is an aesthetic way to present products and services, interest users and, at the same time, abstract them from reality.

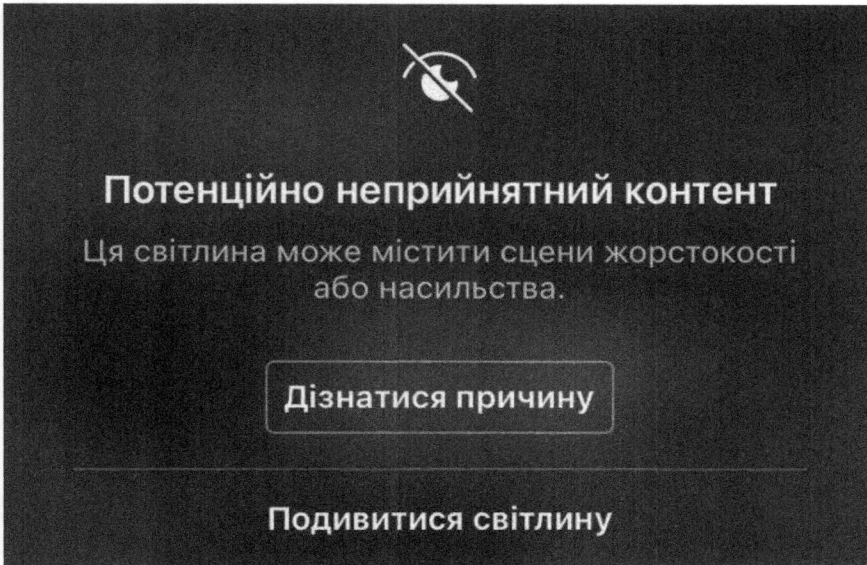

Потенційно неприйнятний контент

Ця світлина може містити сцени жорстокості або насильства.

Дізнатися причину

Подивитися світлину

112 вподобань

tata.ukrainique E40 Highway. russian war crimes against Ukraine's civilian population.
Note the number of female bodies that russian non-humans presumably tried to burn. It is hard to even imagine what these women had gone through before they died. Raped, murdered, burned

When I come out of the basement after the sirens go off, it's completely dark around, but now stars are very visible. The siren is still ringing, and the neighbor's dog is shouting at her for a long time, plaintively. Perhaps a month ago, I would have seen in all of this a clear confirmation of Luciana Parisi's ideas about the technoecologies of sensation. "Changes in technical machines are inseparable from changes in the material, cognitive and affective capacities of a body to feel,"—she wrote. Now everyone feels it in such mediated nervous tremors, dissociations, panic attacks, anxieties and fears, multiplied suffering, inspiration, love, destruction, tenderness, in military units and volunteer graphs, infrastructural spasms — in this high-intensity event: the war.

I notice how my near-theoretical observations seem to me powerless and untimely. I have to do something different for everyone, not waste time on this. I know it's not so unequivocally, but I just feel that way right now. I know it's part of the extension, its human source. Our emotions have become so militarized before the start of this war, that when we try to return to ourselves, it feels like betrayal, guilt, threat.

Ukrainian public intellectual Andriy Baumeister wrote on his Facebook page about the shifts in social psychology during the war, about collective emotionality: "The ideal is when everyone feels 'as one', experiences 'as one'. It is a question of identity and loyalty. My feelings no longer belong to me. [...] A depressed and repressed individuality will experience complex emotions. When each of us will be ashamed of our 'individual' feelings and ask ourselves: is it good, is acceptable, or morally have 'my own' emotions and feelings? Is there no betrayal and moral sin in this?".

When everyone is now a weapon, semi-automatic / semi-human—the desire of the 'individual' is felt as one of the side effects of humanity. I choose to keep it too. Such forbidden little things as just sitting for ten minutes on the street and watching the movement of people or a river; or to smell a blossoming cherry tree; or to write and read alone, when I can, something that does not do any good.

It seems that Ukrainians need to invent a special way to win in cyberwars, where the mental and the physical are not opposed, the rational and the sensual go side by side, where you need to remain deceived and not deceived at the same time, expanding and contracting, automating and humanizing, stay vulnerable—to know where to go and where to return.

March 3 – April 8, 2022

DISPATCHES FROM THE PLACE OF IMMINENCE, PART 10

May 9 – 29, 2022

SVITLANA MATVIYENKO

The war did not end on May 9th. That day Russia celebrated the 77th anniversary of the defeat of Nazi Germany with a large-scale military parade in Moscow's Red Square. To the huge disappointment of the public, there was no promised flying display of the supersonic Tu-160 strategic bombers, nor a so-called 'Doomsday' IL-80 command and control aircraft, which Russia's top leadership, they say, is supposed to board in the event of a nuclear attack, and which it allegedly can withstand. But then, bad weather conditions were listed as an official reason for the mysterious cancellation of the show, although Moscow meteorologists were ready to disperse clouds.[1] Journalists speculated about the Kremlin's fear of sabotage. Given a growing disappointment of the "quite pro-war [and] aggressively pro-war"[2] Russian military with how the Russia-Ukraine war has been conducted, a rumour has it that the Kremlin could not risk the possibility of one of the pilots re-enacting the suicide attack by Soviet WWII hero Nikolai Gastello by directing the plane towards the commander-in-chief overlooking the Victory Day parade. But then, it is only a rumour.

Since 2015, Ukraine has celebrated the Day of Remembrance and Reconciliation—which replaced the Soviet Victory Day—on May 8th, commemorating the day when the Allies of WWII accepted Germany's unconditional surrender of its armed forces and paid tribute to the WWII victims. While Victory Day over Nazism in World War II on May 9th is still a national holiday, it is a quiet day off. When the final surrender terms were signed on the 8th May 1945 in Berlin at 21:20, with the order by the German High Command to cease active operations following at 23:01 Central European time, it was already 00:01 in Moscow. This one second was used by the Soviet government to shift the victory to a different day, signaling its special role in the war and opening the space for its subsequent monopolization of the victory over Nazism, which it has now fully appropriated as a 'Russian'—instead of a 'Soviet—victory, denying participation of other ethnicities. The decision to join the European tradition recognizes the effort of all Allies and shifts the focus from the demonstration of military force, such as during the Victory Day parade in Moscow, to the much-needed work of remembrance and reconciliation.

On May 8th, Zelensky released a black-and-white video[3] that I started watching but then paused indefinitely. I can no longer stomach all these more-and-more beautiful presidential

---

1   m24.ru. (2022, May 6). *В Москве придется разгонять облака для проведения парада Победы – синоптик*. https://www.m24.ru/news/obshchestvo/06052022/458700.

2   Standish, R. (2022, May 8). *Interview: Why The "Failure" Of Russian Spies, Generals Is Leading To "Apocalyptic" Thinking In The Kremlin*. RadioFreeEurope/RadioLiberty. https://www.rferl.org/a/russia-ukraine-war-setbacks-strategy-generals-putin/31839737.html.

3   *Звернення Володимира Зеленського з нагоди Дня пам'яті та примирення*. (2022, May 8). [Video]. YouTube. https://www.youtube.com/watch?v=VTHA4LtYRQ8.

videos. Something important is lost, precisely where he struggles to grasp your attention with that upgraded camerawork and his significantly improved speeches. The video tries to achieve the impossible—speaking to so many different audiences that it feels a little bit schizophrenic. We are burnt-out here, quite literally so. But the rest of the world is bored. Two months. This is how long it can pay attention to a war. When you get on the cover of *Time*, it's about closing the conversation, not anything else. In what I've managed to see in this post-*Time* video, Zelensky stands near a bombed civilian apartment building in Borodianka, a small town in the Bucha region, completely destroyed in Spring 2022, and he goes: "During two years of WWII the Nazis killed 10,000 people in Mariupol... During two months of occupation the Russian army killed 20,000 civilians." A slow camera movement, crawling along the building's ruined wall, is focused on tiny details and textures of torn objects; their assaulted materiality makes me imagine a forced decomposition of life at the high speed of an explosion so that today even the moving image cannot breathe life in this *nature morte*.

The parallels between WWII and this Russian war in Ukraine that Zelensky highlights in the video are, admittedly, beyond uncanny. This resemblance of the Nazis' and the Russians' actions, however, elucidates nothing about Russian troops, instead, it is meant to confuse, by exploiting and assaulting the logic of common sense. "They cannot be fascists and, at the same time, fetishize their victory over fascism in WWII, and also claim they conduct a 'de-nazifying operation' of Ukraine." I am still trying to wrap my head around that, but it's either that the designer of this campaign thought the more the Russian army resemble the Nazi army in their conduct the less its fascist acts would be perceived as such, or, instead, that the resemblance is simply a blunt and straightforward message aiming to shock and intimidate. Or both. Or, perhaps, it's just multiple uncorrelated decision-making fuck ups that desperately need to look like a complex coordinated mission. Whatever it is, this resemblance subverts your abductive reasoning, just like Marx Brothers' joke that Žižek favors, rephrased as: "They may look like fascists and talk like fascists, but don't let that fool you. They really are fascists." This fascism, with all the practices it has pulled out of the archives, is also data-fascism: it puts the subjects through 'filtration' by searching for the signs of *impurity* through citizens' bodies and data on digital devices. It searches for anything that it can use for expanding its power and control—through the land and living tissue. Everything we know about biopolitical regimes of information capitalism has materialize—in its most uncompromisingly forthright form—in the brutality of filtration camps.

There was no general mobilization announced during the Parade in Moscow, instead, a crawling mobilization has been happening for quite some time it seems—in disguise. Journalists report that men in the regions of the Russian Federation have been invited to military enlistment offices under different rationale – for example, to check or correct their service record[4]—where they are asked, sometimes under pressure, to sign military contracts. Not all do, and refusals among the civilians, it seems, are many, since a special stamp has been manufactured and distributed among enlistment offices that is, indeed, used for 'correcting' a military service record of those who do not want to go to war by marking it with

---

4   *Тайная мобилизация. Как россиян забирают на войну.* (2022, May 22). [Video]. YouTube. https://www.youtube.com/watch?v=XRDh3UFPS44.

a shaming note, which reads: "Capable of betrayal, lie, and deception. Refused to participate in the special military operation in LNR, DNR, and Ukraine."[5]

During the first trial of war criminals that began in Ukraine in May,[6] the details were released of how Vadim Shishimarin, a 21-year-old Russian tankunit sergeant, following the order of a senior officer, killed a civilian only because that man on a bike had a cell phone on him and, thus, was assumed to posit a threat to several lost Russian soldiers in the Ukrainian village of Chupakhivka.[7] As Victoria Ievleva, a Russian photographer and journalist who was present during this trial, revealed (10:40) after checking the soldier's record in his city of Ust-Ilimsk in the Irkutsk region, Shishimarin, quite unusually, she says, had 211,000 rubles of utilities debt, which might be among the reasons for him to sign a military contract in 2020, after which, according to the words of his mother, he was happy to live in a barn for free.[8] According to numerous investigations, including reports from Mediazona and Proekt, the Russian forces mostly consist of young people (the age of most killed is 21-23 years old[9]) from the poorest regions of the Russian Federation: Dagestan, Buryatia, as well as the Krasnodar, Orenburg, Stavropol, and Volgograd regions where the Russian Federation mobilized the representatives of the poorest minority ethnic communities, who have been targeted by normalized official discrimination and 'Russification' processes over several long decades—the subjects of imperialism themselves, who proudly identify themselves as 'Russian.' In the end, these subjects of imperialism can only partake in such identification processes as part of the RF army, the discriminatory Other, with whom they are temporarily united to re-enact such violence, the victims of which they and many generations of their families have been for decades. Journalist and human rights activist from Ulan-Ude Yevgenia Baltatarova commented on the existing gap between the center and the periphery of the Russian Federation, Buryatia, that exists partly for economic reasons and partly for reasons of racism. The imperialist mentality is clear even in the discourse of the Russian liberal media and public, she says. Imperialist epistemology is always deep and often subtle, as decades of colonial and postcolonial studies have shown. Yet in the case of the Russian Federation, problematizing the nuances of imperialist patronization of imperial subjects would have allowed one to address what Baltatarova describes as the mindset where "many people live in their small Buryat world. This is the logic of the colony: it is better not to interfere in all these great upheavals. 'White great people' will decide for us. This is their war."[10] My hope is that

5   *Leonid Volkov on.* (2022, April 13). [Tweet]. Twitter. https://twitter.com/leonidvolkov/status/1514199073632444419.

6   Hunder, M., & Balmforth, T. (2022, May 19). *Ukraine prosecutor seeks life sentence for Russian soldier in war crimes trial.* Reuters. https://www.reuters.com/world/europe/russian-soldier-asks-forgiveness-ukraine-war-crimes-trial-2022-05-19/.

7   Lovett, I. (2022, May 23). *The Story Behind Ukraine's First War-Crimes Trial.* WSJ. https://www.wsj.com/articles/why-did-you-do-this-the-story-behind-ukraines-first-war-crimes-trial-11653226541.

8   *Скрытая мобилизация. Суд над российским военным в Украине. Зять Путина — Зеленский. Дорн. Гуриев.* (2022, May 19). [Video]. <YouTube. https://www.youtube.com/watch?v=e5Vzl-zNG1c>.

9   *Потери России в войне с Украиной. Сводка «Медиазоны».* (2022). Медиазона. https://zona.media/casualties.

10   *Солдати невдачі. Чи винні буряти у звірствах в Україні та чи стане Бурятія незалежною – інтерв'ю з опозиціонеркою з Улан-Уде.* (2022). Pravda. https://www.pravda.com.ua/articles/2022/05/27/7348743/.

the decolonization of the Russian Federation, as researchers Botakoz Kassymbekova and Erica Marat wrote, indeed, has already begun with the Russian war in Ukraine.[11] My terror is that there won't be enough time even to launch this complex and monumental project as the realm of such opportunity is closing while the boredom and tiredness with this war clearly seen in the mood of the global public and political establishment and, along with the growing fear of a nuclear threat or famine, have been played well by the Russian state's lobbyists and propaganda, and may well indicate that the world is ready to sacrifice Ukraine.

Some of the military brigades sent to Ukraine have been known for internal violence, often of a racial character, between Slavic and non-Slavic groups, such as the infamous 64th Separate Motor Rifle Brigade from Khabarovsk,[12] who are now known to the whole world for their war crimes in Bucha.[13] On the online forum for the soldiers' and relatives of soldiers from this brigade, a user reported back in 2014 that to escape service and violent treatment there soldiers "ate bleach and swallowed needles." Others, however, proudly recalled that this military unit in the Kniaze-Volkonskoe village of Khabarovsk region, known by its nickname 'Mlechnik,' is 'not for the weak' since 'real men' are made there, and yet others, still back in 2015, were desperately looking for their missing sons.[14] In April 2022, when the 64th Separate Motor Rifle Brigade, accompanied by the also identified 104th and 234th battalions of Pskov's paratroopers,[15] withdrew from the Kyiv region and the atrocities in Bucha, Irpin, Motyzhyn, Borodianka, Makariv were discovered, the last page of this forum is filled in by the posts of Ukrainians—their rage, pain, shock, and death wishes to the invaders. One Ukrainian user posted a link to a Google drive folder with videos and photographs for these so-called 'real men' and their relatives to see.[16] As I read these posts, I know that Ukrainians come to this forum not only to discharge their feelings or inform Russian citizens-in-denial about the events in Ukraine; most of us come here drawn by that same question—'Who are you, what are you, the invader?'

This is naïve, certainly, to hope one can comprehend or, at least, identify a mechanism that turns a mother's 20-year-old boy into a murderous rapist;[17] it is even harder, perhaps, to notice how one turns into a shooter, like Stg. Shishimarin who, without questioning the order, fired at a man just because he "wanted to be left alone." But then, if your propaganda tells you that anyone on a particular territory is a 'Nazi' and subject to being purged, it is much

11   Kassymbekova, B. (2022). *Time to Question Russia's Imperial Innocence – PONARS Eurasia*. Ponars Eurasia. https://www.ponarseurasia.org/time-to-question-russias-imperial-innocence/.

12   Gall, C., & Berehulak, D. (2022, May 23). *'Such Bad Guys Will Come': How One Russian Brigade Terrorized Bucha*. The New York Times. https://www.nytimes.com/2022/05/22/world/europe/ukraine-bucha-war-crimes-russia.html.

13   Gettleman, J. (2022, April 29). *Ukraine Identifies Russian Soldiers in Bucha Atrocities*. The New York Times. https://www.nytimes.com/2022/04/29/world/europe/bucha-russian-soliders-atrocities.html.

14   *Mlechnik* (2022). Esosedi. http://ru.esosedi.org/RU/KHA/8352879/v_ch_51460_mlechnik/.

15   Gettleman, J. (2022b, April 29). *Ukraine Identifies Russian Soldiers in Bucha Atrocities*. The New York Times. https://www.nytimes.com/2022/04/29/world/europe/bucha-russian-soliders-atrocities.html.

16   *Russian War Crimes â Google Drev.* (2022). Google Drive. https://drive.google.com/drive/folders/1-3_RECcAKk5LftVIvGoD6Z8-_9dLJYCa.

17   *Another occupying forces soldier identified as a rapist - Prosecutor General.* (2022, May 17). Pravda. https://www.pravda.com.ua/eng/news/2022/05/17/7346715/.

easier to do so, I suppose. It means there are no accidental civilian killings in this war. Despite how strange it may look to some, it is only logical that the first sentenced—and sentenced for life—war criminal in this brutal war, is not a torturer or rapist or mass-murder, like those already identified by the Ukrainian Security Services and the international teams of investigative journalists, but a young Siberian man with an enormous utility bill—an imperial subject, a non-accidental shooter.[18]

To accelerate the production of troops, the covert mobilization unfolds in the grey zones. Such are the self-proclaimed 'Donetsk and Luhansk Peoples' Republics,' where a refusal to sign contracts is pretty much impossible. Besides, the age limit to serve has been recently increased there from 55 to 65 years. The general understanding is that those mobilized, often armed with Mosin rifles that were in service during the First World War,[19] are typically used as cannon fodder. Even pro-Russian military bloggers criticized the Kremlin "for appalling treatment of forcefully mobilized DNR and LNR servicemen—contradicting Russian information campaigns about progress of the Russian special military operation."[20] Forced mobilization has been also reported in blockaded Mariupol and, for more than two months now, in other occupied territories, including the workers of strategic and critical infrastructure, as well as people with disabilities.[21] Unsurprisingly, the Russian Federation also mobilizes through prisons. Olga Romanova, Russian journalist and founding director of Russia Behind Bars, an NGO Charitable Foundation for Assistance to Convicts and Their Families, reported the mounting cases of contracting convicts with military experience (23:20), who have served in the military or police forces, at least in several Russian prison zones, particularly near the city Nizhniy Tagil in Ural and in the region of Nizhniy Novgorod, where convicts are offered a release from prison if they sign contracts to go to war in Ukraine.[22] Does it look like a 'special military operation' when 21-conscripts and 64-year-old seniors could be mobilized and sent to combat? To me, it looks like war.

They recently said on Russia's state TV that the victory over fascism in WWII was apparently incomplete and the Nazis have been living in Ukraine ever since, which makes the 'special military operation' an extension of WWII that has resurfaced all-unannounced via a twisted temporal fold. Putin has been repeatedly claiming that the invasion was something they "couldn't not commit." "We had no choice," he has been repeating for the cameras, by alluding to the Russian state's urge to supress anyone who attempts installing a border, which threatens its sense of the borderless empire. "If we had at least one chance to solve this

18   *Revealed the murder of the family starosti village of motizhyn.* (2022, May 24). [Text post]. Facebook. https://www.facebook.com/VenediktovaIryna/posts/395188032618871.

19   Hromadske Radio. (2022, May 3). Those mobilized in LNR are armed with rifles from tsarist Russia — military expert. Громадське Радіо. https://hromadske.radio/en/news/2022/05/03/those-mobilized-in-lnr-are-armed-with-rifles-from-tsarist-russia-military-expert.

20   *RUSSIAN OFFENSIVE CAMPAIGN ASSESSMENT.* (2022, May 25). ISW. https://understandingwar.org/backgrounder/russian-offensive-campaign-assessment-may-25.

21   Громадське радіо. (2022, April 10). *В ОРДЛО «мобілізують» інвалідів дитинства і співробітників «стратегічних підприємств» — розвідка.* https://hromadske.radio/news/2022/04/10/v-ordlo-mobilizuiut-invalidiv-dytynstva-i-spivrobitnyky-stratehichnykh-pidpryiemstv-rozvidka.

22   *Скрытая мобилизация. Суд над российским военным в Украине. Зять Путина — Зеленский. Дорн. Гуриев.* (2022b, May 19). [Video]. YouTube. https://www.youtube.com/watch?v=e5VzI-zNG1c.

problem by peaceful means, we would have used this chance, but they did not leave us this chance, did not give it to us, there was simply no other choice," he says again at the meeting with the father of separatist Zhoga, broadcasted on May 9th, as Putin hands him his son's posthumous award.[23] This meeting, where, caught by a shortness of breath, Putin articulates the words with a noticeable effort, is staged to reiterate the sense of *destiny*, which—despite that it screams paranoia—seems to become the only official 'explanation' of the war.

In a Facebook post with the catchy title, 'Motorola' Entered the Kremlin, Russian human rights activist Marina Litvinovich is worried that with such broadcasted meetings the Kremlin has started demonstrating a disturbing closeness with the Donbas separatists. In the post title, she refers to the nickname of one of the early Russian invaders, Arseniy Pavlov, who came to Ukraine in 2014, running from a prison sentence in the RF for stealing a car from a carwash where he worked in Rostov-on-Don, then he joined separatists by organizing his own group 'Sparta,' and eventually became popular for his GoPro videos of the battle for the Donetsk airport shot by the camera stuck on his combat helmet. Later, Pavlov also drew attention with a confession about his personal execution of fifteen prisoners, in a phone interview to a journalist, signaling his utter indifference about the lives taken, some of them after severe torture.[24] And yet, the perception of such people like 'Motorola' is actively changing in Russia. As Litvinovich wrote on May 10th, several regional officials in the RF announced that they started naming streets after the DNR and LNR separatists in eleven cities across the Russian Federation.[25] After years of denying any association with the separatist forces in Donbas, the Federation now inscribes them in the state history: "The Kremlin is no longer ashamed about the downed Boeing and everything that has happened on the territory of the DPR and LPR for all these '8 years'," Litvinovich observes, "and now, after 'this is not us', comes 'this is us.'"

On May 13th, I got my fifth dose of the Covid vaccine: by now, it's two CoronaVac doses plus three Pfizer doses. It may seem overprotective; but actually is not. Two months ago, my friend's husband died of a chronic disease, which became fatal for him after he caught Covid at the hospital. I came to visit her after the funeral, when she, a doctor, got upset about me wearing a mask at her home and asked me to take it off, so I did. There are still signs everywhere warning you not to enter stores and offices without a mask, but if you suddenly see one person in a mask in my town, it would be me. My friend Yevgen, a cytologist, cell biologist, and employee of the Institute of Gerontology in Kyiv, tells me that Covid has certainly disappeared from the news, but the war remains a friendly environment for the virus. There are some unclear dynamics, however, that is yet to be studied. On the one hand, for instance, big gatherings of people—such as in the bomb shelters, refugee

---

23 *Вони мене ставили до стінки розстрілювати – Роман Безсмертний про війну, Росію та життя в окупації.* (2022, May 16). [Video]. YouTube. https://www.youtube.com/watch?v=LVQkVV7UEkA.

24 *Motorola confesses he murdered 15 prisoners. Признание Моторолы в убийстве 15 пленных.* (2015, April 6). [Video]. YouTube. https://www.youtube.com/watch?v=yXSctfYltaM.

25 Litvinovich, M. (2022, May 10). *«МОТОРОЛА» ВОШЁЛ В КРЕМЛЬ* [Text Post]. Facebook. https://www.facebook.com/marina.litvinovich/posts/10160097364269675.

camps, and military training bases—facilitate virus transmission.[26] On the other hand, the imposed curfew that limits communication along with the alcohol ban for an extended time in February and March prevented it. But then, people do not call or go see doctors when they are in danger. Half of the state hospitals are bombed. Many people treat their illness themselves. Many quietly die at home. The scientific lab in Kyiv where Yevgen works, which was partly turned into a diagnostic center during the pandemic, stopped processing tests, he says, since February 24th they have received none. And there was not a single person at the vaccination center, apart from me, either, when I came to get the booster—just a bored young doctor and a nurse, sitting there with their noses in their phones, reading the war news in silence.

Despite the projected escalation, the regions away from the frontlines experienced relatively quiet days after May 9th, which still felt disturbing and was interpreted by many as regrouping and strengthening the invader's army. On May 15th, I woke up at 3:35 am due to the air raid siren, the first one since May 8th in our region. This time the Russian rockets hit Lviv military infrastructure.[27] The Telegram gossip, again, tells us this one is due to Ukraine's victory in the European pop song contest. When several days later I speak with my friend Susanna, feminist media scholar from Finland, unsurprisingly, perhaps, our conversation slides from NATO to Eurovision. "Ah, Eurovision," she notes with that dark humor I appreciate about her way of thinking, "that's how Europe helps." Two weeks later, the winner of Eurovision-2022 Kalush Orchestra sells the Crystal Mic, a symbol of their victory, at the charity auction for 900,000 USD to purchase the PD-2 drone complex for the Ukrainian army, and the crypto community WhiteBIT becomes the new owner of the cup.[28]

---

26   *350 людей у тісному підвалі: спогади волонтерки про 27 днів окупації на чернігівщині.* (2022). Pravda. https://life.pravda.com.ua/society/2022/04/12/248204/.

27   *Вночі російські ракети вдарили по військовому об'єкту на львівщині.* (2022). Pravda. https://www. pravda.com.ua/news/2022/05/15/7346289/.

28   *Компанія WhiteBIT на DOU.* (2022). ДОУ. https://jobs.dou.ua/companies/whitebit/.

On May 18th, when the entire air raid alert map turns read,[29] the Telegram channel of the Russian Ministry of Defence publishes the Statement of the Interdepartmental Coordination Headquarters of the Russian Federation for Humanitarian Response, where my town is mentioned among two others—Kramatorsk in Donbas and Podolsk in the Odesa region – and where, it says, that Ukrainian Neo-Nazis hide their reactive volley fire systems "using hospitals, civilian buildings, schools, kindergartens, and sanatoriums." It reads: "In Kamenets-Podolsk, Khmelnytsky region, in the buildings of the regional children's tuberculosis sanatorium on Sitsinsky Street and the boarding school No. 2 on Lesya Ukrainka Street, Ukrainian Military Force units equipped firing positions, and artillery and the Reactive volley fire systems were located in the adjacent territory. At the same time, the staff of institutions and residents of nearby houses are kept as a 'living shield'."[30] Curiously, the tuberculosis sanatorium and the boarding school No. 2 are no longer in those buildings for at least ten years. One of these historic buildings, with an utterly beautiful pink façade that was built as one of the first school for girls in the region a hundred years ago, is a private lyceum called 'Slavutynka,' and is now hosting school children refugees from Odesa, Chernihiv, and Kyiv. My close friend Nelya works there as a school doctor. Trust me, there are no reactive volley fire systems—it is my jogging route, I would have seen them.

Since that Russian statement was posted, I am scared my town may lose these historical buildings one day due to an air strike. We know through these months of invasion that the Russian state manufactures and publicizes such fakes to justify their forthcoming attacks on civilian infrastructure. I do not know if any measures are applied by the lyceum administration these days to secure kids—Nelya has been on health leave, so she does not know either—but they seem to be open and working, despite the news. Nelya thought this fake was meant to disorient and scare. And yet, I had an urge to walk by the buildings. On May 20th, I asked Nelya to join me. She has chronic pain in her legs, so we walked rather slowly, and I managed, by stretching my arm towards the building, to leave a long but somewhat interrupted finger trail through the entire building's wall—an invisible trail so that only I knew it was there. The wall felt rough, but warmed up by late-afternoon sunrays. Nelya kept telling me about her boys, one of whom, who had served near Kyiv, was leaving for the Eastern Front that evening. I was only half-listening to her—even though her words were important, consumed by this awkward and almost erotic sensation of stroking the 100-year-old stone façade.

For almost a week then, a plane keeps circling above the town. This time I am sure it is our air defense reacting to the same piece of news. Everything in me is alert again, every new noise around is felt by my skin. This acute sensitivity to a soundscape is common. My temporary indifference to alerts is pure tiredness that has now caught many of us in the nets of depression. On May 25th, when I woke up at 4:30 am, I saw an audio message from Milena, my colleague and soundscape theorist, who was passing by my house in Vancouver

29   https://alerts.in.ua.
30   *Заявление Межведомственного координационного штаба Российской Федерации по гуманитарному реагированию от 18 мая 2022 г.* (2022, May 18). Telegraph. https://telegra.ph/Zayavlenie-Mezhvedomstvennogo-koordinacionnogo-shtaba-Rossijskoj-Federacii-po-gumanitarnomu-reagirovaniyu-ot-18-maya-2022-g-05-18.

and recorded the loud street crows "having a baby shower or just arguing." Playing it gave me a sudden sense of closeness with that *other* realm where I belonged, but suddenly an air raid alarm went off on my phone, bringing me back to my reality. This app always starts 3-4 minutes before the city alarms, so I approached the bedroom window and set the recorder to grab my soundscape—for Milena. I admit, and she later agreed, this is one of the most terrifyingly beautiful traces of war, which, as a sound producer I recently met explained to me, is unique in Kamyanets-Podilsky, where its layered sonic composition is engaged with the entire complexity of the city landscape and the valley with the river canyon as a gigantic musical instrument.

The map of a country at war is the cartographic uncanny. The ground moves under our feet and so does our map. It is different every day. One day the map shows more of the free Ukraine, next day it shows less. One day it leads you out of a blockaded city, next day it betrays you and gives you up. All advances and withdrawals of the armed forces cause disorienting folds and twists, so that the subject of the map can find oneself on the opposite side of the border, even while standing still. I keep thinking this as I am listening to a young woman telling me about her dream. We are meeting weekly on Zoom to reconstruct the details of her experience of being removed from the village near Mariupol on March 16th, passed through the filtration process, and subsequently being deported to Russia. From a safe location in Europe where the lucky escape route led her, she tells me, on May 20th, she dreamt about being caught, again, inside the Russian territory with no exit. Just like in the 1930s, for many Ukrainians, the map of the Russian Federation will certainly mean nothing but entrapment, the suffocating memory of which will keep returning as nightmares.

The deportation of Ukrainian citizens to Russia that began before the invasion on February 24th has now drawn over a million people across the border, and the process of removing Ukrainian civilians still continues. There is not much room for resistance when civil and human rights of the subject are suspended. We keep receiving the updates, like this one on May 18th[31]: "Yesterday, 539 Ukrainians, including 55 kids were taken from Mariupol to a village Bezymiane of the Novoazovsky region to Russia where they are placed in the camp while Russian military are preparing them for deportation." In some cases, people are simply kidnapped. Some of them are kept in camps, others in pre-trial detention centers;[32] their destiny, including those who passed the filtration, is equally unclear.

On May 18th, the advisor to Mariupol mayor Petro Andriyshchenko reports that the city is facing an epidemiological catastrophe due to a potential cholera outbreak.[33] The reasons are multiple: from the destruction of the city's critical infrastructure causing a lack of heat

---

31   Hmelnicka, V. (2022, May 18). *Invaders Are Planning Forced Deportations of At Least Five Hundred Mariupol Residents, Including 55 Children*. TCH.Ua. https://tsn.ua/en/ato/invaders-are-planning-forced-deportations-of-at-least-five-hundred-mariupol-residents-including-55-children-2065375.html.

32   Время, Н. (2022, May 18). *"Собирайте документы, мы вас забираем". Гражданских украинцев держат в российских СИЗО*. Настоящее Время. https://www.currenttime.tv/a/ukraintsy-v-sizo-rossii/31856366.html.

33   «Кто не проходит фильтрацию, попадают в концлагерь»: советник мэра Мариуполя о ситуации в городе. (2022, May 18). [Video]. YouTube. https://www.youtube.com/watch?v=zJIbgSKKyBY.

and water to the immense number of unburied bodies, or those buried everywhere in the city often very close to the surface, when people did not have a possibility to dig proper graves between airstrikes and bombing. After the withdrawal of the Ukrainian soldiers from Azovstal, he says, a limited quantity of food and meds was distributed in several parts of the city, but the installment of a heavy military regime in Mariupol with many checkpoints creates a serious threat for civilians. To move around the city, one needs a document for passing the filtration process and a general pass issued based on the former. When people do not pass the filtration process, they are sent to the Yelenovka prison camp, where the Russian forces now keep between 3,000 to 4,000 people from Mariupol. "It is a real concentration camp," Andriyshchenko says.[34] What's left of the city is turning into a commune of survivors, cut off from any communication means, uninformed about the developments of the war. On May 16th, Andriyshchenko reported that the occupants announced a compensation of 500,000 RUB / 6,000 USD for a destroyed home or 3,000,000 RUB / 33,000 for a lost family member, but citizens can only register such a claim if they indicate that the home was destroyed or relative was killed by Ukrainian soldiers.[35]

The procedure of filtration varies in different places; if successful, people receive a note of passing.[36] If the subjects are found to be in opposition to the war—for instance, on social media or in private text messages, they could be forced to record 'public apologies.' The videos of such apologies, are shared online.[37] In this video from occupied Kherson, a Ukrainian woman with a trembling voice is telling on camera that she underwent 'a denazification course,' then she apologizes to the citizens of the Russian Federation and Russian soldiers for calling them 'orks.' In mid-May, there are already over 500 Ukrainian citizens detained in Kherson, who are currently kept in so-called 'torture cellars.' The number of places of captivity in the city is growing. The instances of local collaboration with the occupants multiply, where some citizens help the invaders make lists of activists, politicians, journalists, bloggers, that could be used, under torture, as *material* for propaganda videos. The number of rape cases including the rape of children in the Kherson region also grows.[38] But there is also an active partisan movement, and the ongoing peaceful demonstrations against occupation, in which people march to city squares with Ukrainian flags, that are truly heroic.

On May 24th, I took my mother home after a month at the hospital. Due to the surgery stress, she is showing more visible signs of dementia. I patiently answer the same questions over and over again, day after day. We drew a detailed and clear table of her pill schedule. Every couple of days I explain to her how to use Viber, so she can write or call me when she needs

34   *«Кто не проходит фильтрацию, попадают в концлагерь»: советник мэра Мариуполя о ситуации в городе.* (2022b, May 18). [Video]. YouTube. https://www.youtube.com/watch?v=zJlbgSKKyBY.
35   *Андрющенко Time.* (2022, May 16). [Telegram post]. Telegram. https://t.me/andriyshTime/916.
36   *Українська правда on.* (2022, May 3). [Tweet]. Twitter. https://twitter.com/ukrpravda_news/status/1521513547708211200.
37   *Andrey Zakharov on.* (2022, May 20). [Tweet]. Twitter. https://twitter.com/skazal_on/status/1527569778063335425.
38   Klitina, A. (2022, May 24). *Russian atrocities in Kherson region, rape of children, Ukrainian partisans resisting - KyivPost - Ukraine's Global Voice.* KyivPost. https://www.kyivpost.com/ukraine-politics/russian-atrocities-in-kherson-region-rape-of-children-ukrainian-partisans-resisting.html.

to. Since she's at home, her pain has significantly increased and her ability to walk, regardless of the doctor's projection has , has started slowly decreasing. Despite all of her overwhelming fragility—I am often afraid to even hug her, a bird-looking creature, who lost half of her size over the last decade—she really knows how to hide her pain, and I hope I still have the time to learn this essential skill from her during our time together. Earlier, when I enter my parents' place, she would smile, as her joy of seeing me always overruns the pains she's been living with all this year. But now she does not, and I know it's from a different pain that she cannot repress, mixed with despair and fear. It took her a while, but now she understands how terrible our situation is and she often apologizes to me because I have to be here "because of her." Yesterday, when her dementia suddenly shielded her for a moment from our nightmarish reality, she told me, smiling again, that she has been craving a watermelon from Kherson—"not too long to wait till mid-summer!" There will be no Kherson watermelons this year, mama.

(SOME OF) THE WAYS TO SUPPORT UKRAINE

11111 &23%#719

The initiatives were selected from supportukrainenow.org.
Please visit their website to see more options.

Donate

United24 → u24.gov.ua
Hospitallers → hospitallers.life
Helping to Leave → helpingtoleave.org/en

Join a Protest in Your City

The updating list of protests all around the
world: standwithukraine.live/peace-protests/

Donate Internet Equipment

Keep Ukraine Connected → nogalliance.org/
our-task-forces/keep-ukraine-connected/

Hire Ukrainians

Job Aid Ukraine → jobaidukraine.com

Help Ukrainian Cyberdefense

Hacken Proof → hackenproof.com/ukraine-
will-win/call-for-ukrainian-cyber-defense-
stop-the-war

Preserve Ukrainian Cultural Heritage

Saving Ukrainian Cultural Heritage Online
(SUCHO) → sucho.org

Volunteer or help professionally

Support Ukraine Now (sign-up form) →
bit.ly/3PmmDM4

**The constantly updated list of Ukraine-
support organizations, compiled by the
Oxford University Ukrainian Society:**

NOTES ON CONTRIBUTORS

11111 &23%#719 is a contemporary art worker.

Elmaz Asan is a Crimean Tatar/Ukrainian journalist (ATR Channel, Kyiv, Ukraine) and activist. She made a number of documentaries on the past and present of Crimean Tatar people (entitled 'Those Who Open the Way to the Homeland....' and 'Who are Crimean Tatars?'); she (co-)produced TV-programmes and represented the Crimean Tatar journalist network at international conferences. Asanova graduated from Taras Shevchenko Kyiv National University and works on a PhD thesis dedicated to the development of religious and secular education in early-20th century Crimea. Since April 2022, she has been a journalist-in-residence in NIAS, Amsterdam.

Franco 'Bifo' Berardi is an Italian communist philosopher, writer, artist, theorist, and activist in the autonomist tradition, whose work mainly focuses on the role of the media and information technology within neoliberal financial capitalism. He is the founder of the famous 'Radio Alice' in Bologna, and the magazine *A/traverso*. His books are translated into many languages. This is a short, selected list of the most recent ones: *The Second Coming* (Polity, 2019), *Breathing* (Semiotext(e)/Intervention Series, 2018), *Futurability - The Age of Impotence and the Horizon of Possibility* (Verso, 2017), and *Phenomenology of the End* (Semiotexte, 2016).

Andrii Dostliev (b. 1984) is an artist, curator, and photography researcher from Ukraine, currently based in Poland. He has degrees in IT and graphic design. His primary areas of interest are memory, trauma, identity—both personal and collective, and the limits of photography as a medium. His art practice encompasses photography, video, drawing, performance, and installation. He has published several photo books.

Lia Dostlieva (1984, Donetsk, Ukraine) is an artist, cultural anthropologist, and essayist. Primary areas of Lia's research include the issues of trauma, postmemory, commemorative practices, and agency and visibility of vulnerable groups. Lia is particularly interested in how trauma comes to language, in the possibilities of representation of traumatic events, and in how 'difficult knowledge' and 'difficult past' could be described and visualized. As an artist, Lia works across a wide range of media including photography, installations, textile sculptures, and interventions into urban space since 2012.

Olexii Kuchanskyi is an independent researcher, art & queer writer, whose main interests lie in the experimental moving image art, its ecological impact, and critical cultures of nature. S/he was born in Vinnytsia, Ukraine. S/he lives in Lviv–Kyiv. His/her works have been published in *Prostory, Your Art, TransitoryWhite, Political Critique, East-European Film Bulletin, Arts of Working Class, Moscow Art Magazine, e-flux Notes, transversal,* and others.

Karyna Lazaruk (Lviv, Ukraine) is a Berlin-based infographic maker at the NGO Institute of Mass Information. Karyna has a master's degree in Media Communications (Ukrainian Catholic University, 2015). Karyna is also a founder and producer of *Mediiology*, a digital platform that focuses on new media critique, feminism, and thinking of new forms of human well-being in the challenges of today's world.

Geert Lovink is a Dutch media theorist, internet critic, and author of *Uncanny Networks* (2002), *Dark Fiber* (2002), *My First Recession* (2003), *Zero Comments* (2007), *Networks Without a Cause* (2012), *Social Media Abyss* (2016) and *Sad by Design* (2019). In 2003 he received his PhD from the University of Melbourne, followed by a postdoc position at the University of Queensland. In 2004 he founded the Institute of Network Cultures at the Amsterdam University of Applied Sciences. From 2004-2012 he was an associate professor in the new media program of Media studies at the University of Amsterdam. In 2005 and 2006 he was a fellow at the Institute of Advanced Study in Berlin. Between 2007 and 2017 he taught at the European Graduate School (Saas-Fee/Malta) where he supervised five PhD students. In December 2021, Geert Lovink was appointed Professor of Art and Network Cultures at the Art History Department, Faculty of Humanities of the University of Amsterdam. The Chair (one day a week until September 2026) is supported by the Amsterdam University of Applied Science.

Lera Malchenko is a journalist and artist from Ukraine. Lera is part of the collective 'fantastic little splash' and founder of research/media/art project 'Supermova' and is interested in the impact of emerging media on human interactions and collective online practices.

Svitlana Matviyenko is Assistant Professor of Critical Media Analysis in the School of Communication. Her research and teaching are focused on information and cyberwar; political economy of information; media and environment; infrastructure studies; STS. She writes about practices of resistance and mobilization; digital militarism, dis- and misinformation; Internet history; cybernetics; psychoanalysis; posthumanism; the Soviet and the post-Soviet techno-politics; nuclear cultures, including the Chernobyl Zone of Exclusion. She is a co-editor of two collections, *The Imaginary App* (MIT Press, 2014) and *Lacan and the Posthuman* (Palgrave Macmillan, 2018). She is a co-author of *Cyberwar and Revolution: Digital Subterfuge in Global Capitalism* (Minnesota UP, 2019), a winner of the 2019 book award of the Science Technology and Art in International Relations (STAIR) section of the International Studies Association and of the Canadian Communication Association 2020 Gertrude J. Robinson book prize.

Maria Plichta comes from Łódź, Poland. Upon graduating from the Cultural Studies programme at the University of Łódź, she moved to the Netherlands, where she completed a Research MA in Media Studies at the University of Amsterdam. Currently, she works as a PhD researcher at the University of Amsterdam, working on a project about conspiracy theories in Central and Eastern Europe.

Ellen Rutten is a professor of literature and chair of the Department of Russian & Slavic Studies at the University of Amsterdam. At the Amsterdam School for Cultural Analysis, she co-founded and co-coordinate the research collectives 'Digital Emotions and Literature of the 21st Century.' She also acts as editor-in-chief of the journal *Russian Literature*. Her research interests include post-Soviet literature, (Russian and global) art and design, social media, Soviet memory, and nation branding.

Maria van der Togt is an obsessive gatherer—of people, PDFs, and answers. She is an amateur librarian and initiator of a community shadow library at the Sandberg Institute. Her work revolves around the creative potentials and pitfalls of the tools that allow us to gather online, constantly questioning the context-specific, social-technical codes and practices involved in these processes. How can we challenge ourselves and our tools? She is actively trying to figure it out. *(And likes it when people reach out to her.)*

Marc Tuters is a longtime painter and occasional curator who works as a senior lecturer at the University of Amsterdam's Media Studies department where his current research examines radical visual subcultures at the bottom of the Web together with colleagues at the Open Intelligence Lab as well as the Digital Methods Initiative.

Michał 'rysiek' Woźniak is the Information Security Officer at ISNIC, the .is DNS registry. He comes from a tech, policy, and activism background. Before joining ISNIC he was the Chief Information Security Officer at OCCRP and has managed a free-software-focused NGO. He has cooperated with a number of EU-based organizations working in the digital human rights area and participated in several internet governance meetings. His main policy interests include information security, privacy in the digital age, internet governance (including censorship, surveillance, and Net Neutrality), copyright reform, and digital media literacy; rysiek co-authored the *Net Neutrality Compendium*, and the *Media and Information Competencies Catalogue*. He co-founded the Technical Error Correction Collective.